Smart Saving Tips

Jane Furnival

HAY HOUSE

Australia • Canada • Hong Kong • India
South Africa • United Kingdom • United States

First published and distributed in the United Kingdom by:
Hay House UK Ltd, 292B Kensal Rd, London W10 5BE.
Tel.: (44) 20 8962 1230; Fax: (44) 20 8962 1239.
www.hayhouse.co.uk

Published and distributed in the United States of America by:
Hay House, Inc., PO Box 5100, Carlsbad, CA 92018-5100.
Tel.: (1) 760 431 7695 or (800) 654 5126;
Fax: (1) 760 431 6948 or (800) 650 5115. www.hayhouse.com

Published and distributed in Australia by:
Hay House Australia Ltd, 18/36 Ralph St, Alexandria NSW 2015.
Tel.: (61) 2 9669 4299; Fax: (61) 2 9669 4144.
www.hayhouse.com.au

Published and distributed in the Republic of South Africa by:
Hay House SA (Pty), Ltd, PO Box 990, Witkoppen 2068.
Tel./Fax: (27) 11 467 8904.
www.hayhouse.co.za, orders@psdprom.co.za

Published and distributed in India by:
Hay House Publishers India, Muskaan Complex,
Plot No.3, B-2, Vasant Kunj, New Delhi – 110 070.
Tel.: (91) 11 41761620; Fax: (91) 11 41761630.
www.hayhouse.co.in

Distributed in Canada by:
Raincoast, 9050 Shaughnessy St, Vancouver, BC V6P 6E5.
Tel.: (1) 604 323 7100; Fax: (1) 604 323 2600

A catalogue record for this book is available from the British Library.

ISBN 978-1-4019-1540-7

Printed in Great Britain by Cromwell Press.

Acknowledgements

This book is a progression of my earlier book, *Smart Spending with Jane Furnival: You CAN save £1000 in Four Weeks*. I'm delighted to have the chance to thank again all who helped me with that, especially: Ruth Higham; Christine Northam, counsellor for Relate; Dr Cosmo Hallström, Consultant Psychiatrist; Francis Lilley, Cognitive Behavioural Therapist; Anne Redstone, spokesperson for the Chartered Institute of Taxation; and Nicola Ibison at NCI Management.

It is lovely when your regard for people increases the more you work with them. My Dream Publisher Award, in a new format with added bells and whistles, goes to Hay House. Specific Dream Bunny prizes go to editor Michelle Pilley, text editor Ali Nightingale, designer Leanne Siu, Jo Burgess for publicity, and Megan Slyfield for her support.

Official Wonderful Women are Jacqueline Burns, my literary agent at Free Agents, and my TV agent Kirsty McLachlan. Their support, knowledge, wisdom and advice are invaluable.

Special Prizes for Helpfulness at Short Notice must go to Lisa Taylor at Moneyfacts.co.uk, to Jon Bellamy at the Country Gentlemen's Association and to HM, a professional gentleman who gave his advice without wanting a reward.

Andy Dale appeared like a knight on a white charger, to take over the running of my website, *www.smartsavingtips.co.uk*. He is awesomely efficient.

Good Homework Stars go to my husband, Andy Tribble, and son, Charlie Tribble, for making tea and feeding the animals to let me get on; and to Henry Tribble for his forbearance while I have worked. Normal Rupert Bear and Professor Branestawm bedtime reading will now resume (well, do you expect a thrift expert to read her children new books when she has perfectly good old ones?)!

Princess the Head Hen. Ella the cat. Boo, my brilliant Bouvier des Flandres dog. Nothing – not anything – can I write without the comforting knowledge that you are patiently waiting by my feet. Or on them, in certain cases.

The Old Rectory, Cheam Village, 2007.

Contents

Preface

I hope that you will keep this little book around you, and dip into it at odd moments. You will find it useful, whether you want to save a few pounds or a few thousand.

The term 'thrift guru', coined to describe me by BBC1 after I presented their primetime TV series *Smart Spenders*, conjures a picture of me sitting cross-legged on a cushion, intoning advice like 'Stay chilled – all will be well'.

Don't worry – it's nothing like my life or my advice, which are both down-to-earth and full of emotion – optimism, hope, frustration, and sometimes anger at the ways of big financial institutions which ignore fair play and pass over loyal customers in order to offer the best deals to newcomers. Money has tremendous power and arouses great passion.

I use my money-saving skills to the full every day - and learn new ones constantly. Because, unlike any other person writing about saving money that I know of, I'm a full-time working mother with an unemployed husband, a big house bought in better times, and sons aged six, 15 and 20.

I never give advice that I haven't followed myself. I help you for life, with simple suggestions you can follow again and again. I haven't time for fiddly tips like 'Swap credit cards every two weeks' or 'Get six extra points on your supermarket loyalty card this Friday by buying shampoo between 2 and 5pm.'

I give sensible ideas, facts, figures and contact details, which you can do at two in the morning when you wake up, worried about what's in tomorrow's postbag. (Yes, I've been there too.)

I LOVE passing on the stuff that no one else will tell you. It's my 'thing'. For instance, a friend of mine, a senior forensic scientist, was researching whether you could trace the route someone had travelled in a car by analysing what kind of petrol they put in their tank along the way: ecological, super-clean, go-on-longer or whatever. He analysed what went into tankers at refineries and what came out of pumps at various petrol stations. He confided to me that he had now given up both his original idea and, personally, buying premium petrol: he had found too many things that went wrong. I merely pass on this story as an interesting one. I am sure that things have changed since, and that all petrol suppliers are duly diligent. You'll find petrol-saving hints later in this book.

My style of money-saving is summed up by this approach. You CAN have the things that really matter to you, if you understand that you can't have it ALL. Concentrate on the core things you really want, and don't waste money or effort on anything else. Focus. Play as a sportsman does, to win. For instance, I love a nice home where I can live all the time. I am not so interested in long-haul holidays as I don't want to spend a month's mortgage to travel for a day then cram into one or two rooms with my family. YOU may feel the opposite. It doesn't matter what your goal is – just that you know it and pursue it. Here are some general bits of advice to kick off:

- Don't confuse money-saving with buying the cheapest all the time. Buy a few things that last a long time.

- Never muddle the idea of saving money with meanness to others who have less than you. Be mean to yourself, privately. We use salt in the bath, but leave gift bath stuff for guests.

- Don't swagger-shop – that means show off how much you are spending, as if money is no object and spending loads makes you think you're a more important person. It is bad taste and also unfashionable. Quiet good taste is the thing to aim for.

- Swap shopping lists with a friend and compete with each other for who can bring in the whole list for under the given budget. If you want to be savage, agree that the loser does the winner's washing up or other boring chore. THAT should sharpen up your will to win next week…

- If you think you are addicted to shopping, carry a small notepad around. If you buy anything, write down what it is, the price – and how you felt at the time. Happy? Sad? Lonely? What had happened to make you that way? After a week, analyse your crunch-points. To know yourself is to be able to control yourself, with any luck. (Sorry, in this book, we don't buy into the 'Silly me, I'm so loveable but I just can't control my handbag habit' school of behaviour and neither do the bankruptcy courts. Do you want to save money or what?)

- Book yourself up solid in advance, at times when you are tempted to go shopping.

- Never: buy extra stuff in a filling station shop when paying for petrol (average spend on nothing much, nearly £30); go to bargain outlets just because you think that type of spending 'doesn't count'; or go to a supermarket before 2pm when they start marking stuff down.

- Men, don't buy tools. Use the ones you have, or sell them.

- Girls, before being tempted to buy a new outfit, check your wardrobe – you probably have something similar.

- If shopping, take Uncle Mort or any grumpy

old man who can't stand shops. Failing that, take a baby or toddler shopping, as you can't manoeuvre the buggy up and down stairs and they soon get bored.

These are enough tips to be going on with….

Christmas is a particularly difficult time for anyone who wants to save money – and it has been a crunch-time for me twice.

I was never interested in saving money until 1991, when my then-employer, *The European* newspaper, went bust, leaving me heavily pregnant and owed thousands in pay and expenses.

It was Christmas, my husband had recently started his own business, and we had no spare money. We were on the verge of bankruptcy. To find a gift for our eldest son, then a small boy, we went to the local dump. An old pram found there transformed my life. We made it into an old-fashioned go-kart – and I found then that there are ways of living cheaply without living miserably.

Christmas 2006 brought back that time to me. My husband lost his job when his business partner fired him with three months' pay and nothing else – no payment for his shares in a profitable business. It was a shock to be ousted from one's own successful company after 16 years – a business started in an attic with such egalitarian ideals and hope, when we had all put our houses up as guarantees for a bank loan and I had periodically worked for nothing as receptionist.

Now there would never be another Christmas bonus nor valuable perks like BUPA for the children. And among the Christmas cards came a steady stream of lawyers' letters from our own and the other side, including some amazing revelations, and equally eye-watering bills.

Since then, I have coped with a traumatised husband, our sons, a dog, two cats, and a beautiful rambling home which we had recently bought with the aim of doing it up. As I write, we are en route to the High Court and an employment tribunal, with staggering bills.

When every penny counts, food snobbery goes out of the window first. You walk past M&S, with its fruit at up to 50p a piece – not a treat to indulge in now – and fall in love with the local greengrocer or Food Centre where you get five fragrant peaches, a bit bashed, but £1 the lot. You learn to bless New Zealand for its wonderful frozen lamb, often half-price. You find you can do without meat, or feed the family on bacon pieces, and you're delighted with toothpaste at 26p from Boots or supermarkets. You thank God for porridge, so cheap and filling, and wonder why tinned peaches are 16p but tinned apricots cost more.

That Christmas Day, I fed us with a frozen chicken, bought rock-bottom cheap at Iceland just before the shop shut for Christmas Eve. It wasn't half-bad. I pulled up parsnips from the garden and we had our sack of rice from Costco warehouse club.

My husband and I agreed not to give each other gifts, but our youngest son, aged six, cried when he saw just three presents for him on Christmas morning – one from us and one from each of his brothers.

I thought of the thousands of people who were also having to cope in desperate situations, especially those whose Christmas savings were swallowed up in the hamper savings club scandal of the year.

Fortunately we had eggs from my own dear live hens. Instead of a Christmas gift, our family and friends loved home-made lemon cake, yellow from the fresh yolks, or my elderflower cordial, frozen from the previous summer.

I have also discovered how decent, generous and positive most people are, when you are faced with a personal and financial crisis.

Richard Greenfield gave us invaluable expert advice about company procedures and accounting methods, free and from friendship. Juliet Bawden of Dixcot Locations suggested hiring out our sitting room for photography – and it has been a lifesaver (see more on how anyone can do this later on in the book). David and Barbara Nadel, Jacqui Bakunowicz and Penny Beaumont produced glorious Christmas food and luxuries. Ruth Higham and I took our children to the huge slides at Tate Modern for free, instead of to pantomimes…I spent all that Christmas crying, for one reason or another. But here we are, bloody but unbowed and still in my beloved home.

That's what I mean. In this book, you don't get a lot of dry suggestions. This is stuff to help you 'do your life' as my friend Peter Clark calls it.

I'm handing you the tools you need. Here is hope. Never expect happiness – that only comes in moments you're least expecting it. Aim for contentment, which is do-able. Perhaps I'm more of a guru than I thought.

Introduction

Everybody wants to save money. And, these days, everyone needs to. If you would like to make your money go further, or have trouble making ends meet, it is pointless feeling ashamed to admit it. We're all in the same boat today.

It does not mean that you are a bad person or a failure. You are actually a success – because you are taking steps to remedy the problem by reading this book. And I will sort out your problems as painlessly as possible!

I aim to show you quick, practical ways to save money that you can dip in and out of – depending what your particular problems are when it comes to saving and spending.

The Problem

It has never been quicker or easier to get into debt. Increased taxes, rocketing house costs and massive motoring fines chomp away at our hard-earned money like caterpillars eating cabbage. An entire family's weekly food budget can be wiped out when you get an £80 fine for something trivial like driving in an empty bus lane that you didn't notice. It's ridiculous.

On top of this come unexpected expenses: unemployment, illness, setting up home or a new business, parenthood, single parenthood or retirement. Of course, some people do buy too many things too ...

Economists claim that interest rates would have to halve, to help many of us repay our borrowings sensibly, rather than just plod along repaying the interest and waiting for Father Christmas to repay the lot. That drop in interest rates isn't going to happen. In fact, the cost of borrowing is the highest that it has been for six years – and credit cards can cheerfully charge interest of three or four times the Bank of England's base rate.

Each home owes an average of £8,816 – or £54,771 including a mortgage, according to the latest figures. And that debt increases by £13 a day. (Source: Credit Action.)

The average child costs £23.50 daily until he or she reaches 21. The average home costs £30 a day to run. The average car costs £15 a day to run. The average graduate debt is £13,252. Even the over-70s still carry debt – an average mortgage of £37,000.

I'm not going to scare you with the number of people who now become bankrupt each day. We won't go there. Because you won't need to, after doing what I say.

Here, you will find hundreds of names and contact details of organisations that save you money in every way, and even help you earn a few extra pounds without too much bother. Plus loads of facts you didn't know, that will help you become comfortably off.

This is no ordinary book. It's an investment in your future, and your family's.

The checklist that follows is based on the experience of lots of people from debt advisors to self-help debt groups – people who are probably well-in at the deep end compared to you. So don't feel overwhelmed. You will be delighted to find how quickly and easily you can turn your life around.

How seriously are you out of control with your spending?

1.	Did your parents have problems with debt?	Yes/No
2.	If you are feeling low, do you go shopping?	Yes/No
3.	Once you start spending, do you feel powerless to stop?	Yes/No
4.	By spending, do you feel you are making yourself more acceptable to others?	Yes/No
5.	When spending, do you 'compartmentalise' other debts, as if they are not there, and tell yourself that you will pay everything off overnight when your lucky break happens?	Yes/No

6.	Have you spent more in the past two years?	Yes/No
7.	If you do receive unexpected extra money, do you buy something rather than paying off existing credit cards?	Yes/No
8.	Does your shopping make your home life unhappy and cause disagreements?	Yes/No
9.	Do you hide bills from your partner or family?	Yes/No
10.	Have other people commented on your spending?	Yes/No
11.	After spending money, do you feel guilty?	Yes/No
12.	Are your credit card balances increasing but your income staying the same?	Yes/No
13.	Are you paying basic expenses like food or fuel by credit card, because you don't have the cash?	Yes/No
14.	Can you only afford to pay the minimum towards your credit card bills each month?	Yes/No
15.	Are all your credit cards near the limit?	Yes/No
16.	Are you dipping into savings or retirement funds to pay bills?	Yes/No
17.	Are you working overtime, or at a second job, and still not paying off more than the minimum of your credit card bills?	Yes/No
18.	Are you too scared to work out how much you owe?	Yes/No
19.	Do you take a long time to open bills, or never open them?	Yes/No

20.	Have you received a bailiff's letter, court summons or justified debt collection agency letter?	Yes/No
21.	Do you sometimes feel that you are so much in debt that you might as well spend more and enjoy yourself until it all catches up with you?	Yes/No
22.	Does the stress of having debts make you lose sleep or worry, so you can't concentrate during the day?	Yes/No
23.	Do you fear what others might say if they knew how much debt you are in?	Yes/No
24.	Have you ever got drunk or taken drugs to relieve the stress of feeling in debt?	Yes/No
25.	Have you ever lied to get credit?	Yes/No
26.	Have you applied for new loans to pay off your old ones, without considering whether you could afford the interest rate?	Yes/No
27.	Have you considered running away, going bust or suicide because of your debts?	Yes/No

If you answer 'yes' to three or more questions up to and including question 9, you have a moderate problem.

From 9-19, you'll be fine, but only after I have tied you to a tree and duffed you over a bit.

From question 20 onwards, if you answer 'yes' to anything, I urge you to read what I say and try it for a few weeks.

You are not alone. About a third of us lose an hour's sleep a night, worrying about paying bills. (Source: Survey, Orange, 2005.)

You did not run up bills overnight, and the solution won't happen overnight either. You are working on solving the problem. You can only do your best. When you chip away at something, sooner or later, a big chunk will fall.

If you do as I say … You will be richer, happier and sleep better by the end of this book! (And have better sex as a result, if you're lucky.)

If you do even some of what I say, you can save money immediately and stay richer for the rest of your life.

I'm not an airy-fairy theorist who doesn't know how hard it can be to save money. Nor am I a grey, self-satisfied and dreary maths brainbox. I ogle gorgeous things in magazines, and struggle with my self-control in shops. I can't stand minimalism, empty rooms and empty lives, and no one is happier to have a glass of champagne and open a box of chocolates, preferably fresh cream truffles.

But stuff – whatever it is – is only worth having if you can afford it. If you can't, you will feel very low. You might even go bust and lose the lot.

Why am I so certain I can help you? Because I first tried these techniques on myself, when I was left penniless and heavily pregnant after my employer went broke. I use them all the time to help support my family of three children, now that my husband has lost his job. They work for me and they work for others. I have helped people to save hundreds of pounds in as little as three weeks, and some have saved over a thousand.

One of the problems with over-spenders is that they have more than their fair share of charm. That is how others around them let them get away with their endless 'presents' to themselves. When I was the thrift consultant on the series *Smart Spenders*, the families featured would show me around their homes and, as the evidence of extraordinary amounts of overspending came to light, they fluttered their eyelashes, expecting me to let them off the hook and say they could go on with their 'naughty' habits.

Of course, I never did. When I had straightened them out, and told them what to give up and cut out, I think they all went through about ten days of resentment and anger with me.

I didn't care what they thought. I didn't need them to like me – I've got friends to do that. My attitude was that if they needed to be scared witless and needed some very tough talking to shock them into facing financial reality, so be it.

Then something magical happened. They all started saving. Then they began smiling and welcomed my visits. By the end of a month, some were incredibly high on success, bubbling with a new energy and determination. They had rediscovered life beyond materialism and felt free of their worry, sometimes for the first time in years. They were having more sex – they had more time to have sex, as they weren't at the shops or exhausted from shopping! – because they felt better personally, and closer as couples. This could be you.

Thrift – an old-fashioned word for saving money – is nothing to do with meanness towards others. It is a re-balancing of your life so that you don't automatically head for the shops because you need new things.

Of course, I won't be there swinging my leopard-skin handbag and stamping my red stilettos to check up on you as I was on the TV – you hope! But if you do what I say – even half-properly – you will save money quickly.

This book is for general information. The facts contained in it are accurate to the best of my knowledge. I am a thrift expert, not a professional financial adviser and I am not giving you investment, tax, legal or other forms of advice. You must rely on yourself or get personal independent professional advice when making or not making decisions for your own situation.

Making a new start

Start today. You will feel better immediately. If you put it off, you will feel worse as you have now wasted good money on this book, to add to all the rest of your spending – and that is a shame, as I know I can help you.

You may not be a big spender in the sense of splashing out £300 on a bottle of vodka in a club, driving a Maserati or buying a Gucci bag to match each outfit. But if you're reading this book, the chances are that you know you could be spending a lot less and saving a lot more than you do at the moment.

Most people keep a watch over their spending in many areas, but have specific 'problem' areas where their emotions overrule their common sense, and suddenly their wallet flies open. These emotions could be pride, guilt or good old-fashioned self-indulgence.

Take guilt. Many women will know it. An eminent lawyer I know works hard, and seems a sensible person. But in her lunch breaks, she shops at over-priced touristy shops buying trinkets for her children.

Her behaviour means that no present is special to her children. Gifts are everyday occurrences, so she then has to spend super-duper sums of money for birthdays and Christmas.

There are also people who have swallowed a self-love manual and need to 'reward' themselves by buying flimflam all the time, as if they were martyrs or doing us all a favour by just getting through the day. To them I say: the world's work is mainly done by people who aren't 'feeling good about themselves' that day – but manage without buying themselves presents.

If any of the above sounds like you, don't worry. That was then. Don't waste time beating yourself up (or reproaching your partner) about past regrets and extravagance. This is now.

Don't expect yourself to be perfect or you will never start, but instead just sit there fantasising about a future golden time when everything will be OK.

Aim to be 'good enough' and you will achieve your goal. Take your goal seriously, though.

I have also experienced 'clients' who say that they are just on the verge of a business breakthrough and need not heed my advice. I say: Well, take my advice until your ship comes in.

You are also unlikely to become a well-paid footballer or marry the same, especially if you are a lap-dancer who reveals all to a Sunday paper. So stop dreaming.

This is not about denying yourself all treats and luxuries. A little of what you fancy does you good. However, if you feel like a treat, make it a small and cheap one, even if it is symbolic of your future aspirations. Before I bought my first car years ago, I bought a red Dinky toy and put it on my desk while I saved up for the deposit. Have a chocolate, cookie, tin of beer or whatever, but don't have the whole lot at once.

Don't go on a 'last-ever' spending spree just before you begin. This is not a golden opportunity to acquire a suntan machine, set of fondue forks and remote-control Dalek. The following story is a tough analogy but I will make it anyway. A friend of mine decided to give up smoking and before she started, smoked her way through her considerable store of cigarettes three at a time. She became more hooked on nicotine than ever, never gave up and died of throat cancer, aged 52.

Take one day at a time. Concentrate just a little ahead. Think of yourself as playing a game, to win. Tell yourself that if you feel like splashing out, you will do it tomorrow. And tomorrow. Do your best to avoid temptation. But if you fail today, don't throw in the towel. Like a rider falling off a horse, get back on that beast and master it immediately before you lose your nerve.

Get a friend to act as a mentor and monitor your savings at an agreed time each week. Not your nicest friend, nor a bubble-head, but someone you feel a little scared of. You might even need two friends: one mentor and one checker-upper at the end of the week. One to confide in and one to be tough. Or one to hold you and one to hit you. Arrange a specific time to discuss your progress. That gives you a target time to work towards, where you can take stock of how the week has gone, and someone to impress, to give you a pat on the back. Otherwise just make sure you sit down with yourself to take stock once a week.

Tell people what you are doing. Ask for their support in not suggesting shopping trips. Friends or family members who say, 'What the heck? Just give up,' when you are having the slightest difficulty, don't have your best interests at heart. You can email me at *janechapel2@yahoo.co.uk* or through my websites, *www.smartspending.co.uk* and *www.smartsavingtips.co.uk*.

You may only have one or two problem areas to tackle. Here's how to find out.

How to budget

The personal budget planner

Here is my personal budget planner. It will give you a good overview of where your money is going and therefore how you can save more of it. You have instantly saved a fortune on computerised budget planners which are no more than glorified checklists. This one is designed to give you a good overall impression of where your money goes every month.

You can achieve goodish cuts by just figuring out these seven biggest bills and work on cutting them. In most cases, they are your mortgage, transport, entertainment, gas, electricity, phone and food. You could add in absolutely everything you spend. For a copy of a more detailed budget planner, see the Appendix at the back of the book.

How to use this planner

Fill the planner in quickly, rather than putting it off until you retrieve your bank statements and check them off. Later, you can check your guesstimates against your real spending via your bank statement. It will probably be revealing.

Jane's absolutely and totally golden rule, so golden it should be platinum:

'If you lie, you are only cheating yourself'.

Look at your budget sheet. Take a pencil (always use one if possible: it's cheaper than a pen) and halve every figure on it, apart from utilities, insurance, pension payments and mortgage. We'll deal with those later.

Now go through it again. Rub out the halved figures and halve them again.

Now show your cutbacks to your partner, friends or family, and get their comments. It may be more productive for you to suggest their cutbacks, and vice versa.

The Personal Budget Planner

COSTS	£ expenditure per month
Mortgage	
Council tax	
Credit card/Store card payments	
Loan repayments (incl. loans from friends and family)	
Water rates	
Gas	
Electricity	
Landline telephone	
Mobile phone	
Internet connection/dial-up fees	
TV licence/rental	
Cable/Satellite/Digital fees	
Life Insurance	
Pension contributions	
Car Tax	
1	
2	
Car Insurance	
1	
2	

Car MOT/maintenance	
1	
2	
Car running costs	
Train/bus fares/season tickets	
Childcare costs e.g.:	
<ul><li>Nanny/aupair plus their living costs</li><li>Nursery fees</li><li>Pre-school fees</li><li>Private school fees</li><li>Tutor fees</li><li>Student loans</li></ul>	
Clothing	
Beauty/Hair/Spa treatments (incl. products)	
Housekeeping	
Food	
Pets	
Socialising	
Holidays	
The bottom line total	**£................**

There you have it – your general monthly expenditure. Hopefully less than your monthly income.

This level of honesty will enable you to see which areas need to be cut back and also pinpoint flashpoints for further attention. If you need extra copies of the budget planner, you can find a printable version at *www.smartspending.co.uk* or *www.smartsavingtips.co.uk*.

You might like to complete two planners – one with your real figures and the other with revised target figures. Just slashing a few pounds off three or four of the items, especially the luxuries, will greatly affect the bottom line and there is nothing more satisfying than beating your target.

If your expenditure is way ahead of your income and you feel overwhelmed, there are several debt counselling organisations that might be able to help. Never do nothing. Seek advice sooner rather than later, as debt soon escalates and ruins lives.

Beware of private or professional debt/loan companies who charge extortionate interest rates and often resort to unpleasant methods of doing business when they want their money back. See the list of consumer advice associations on page 136.

Keep it real. Debt counselling agencies get fed up with people in debt who persist in thinking it's OK to allow themselves £100 a month for their mobile phones and £200 on nights in the pub.

If you can't complete the budget planner, get someone else to do it for you.

At this point you may have an argument. If you need someone to resolve it, email me at *janechapel2@yahoo.co.uk*. Use this for good, never for evil …

Press on regardless – or you have wasted your money on this book and the opportunity to deal once and for all with your debts.

The sacrifice section

Decide what you don't need

When helping my TV clients to cut back, I removed many people's 'absolute necessities' for a month (i.e. the usual old self-indulgent rubbish like expensive hair conditioner, new trainers, golf-clubs…you name it). They realised they didn't need them at all and didn't want them back.

Do you need several mobile phones? Can you put teenagers on pay-as-you-go contracts and make them responsible?

Check your TV if you have cable or digital. Do you need film channels? Cut out the extra at least for a little. You can go back later.

Nights at the pub. You don't need to buy everyone else a round. Show them this book. Ask them to buy the drinks.

If you want to become a smart saver, you must think around the problem. There is always a way of getting what you want.

> **Top Tip!** If you pay for lunch at the office each day, and you can't bear to give it up every day, take sandwiches three days out of five. You will look forward to your 'days off' more.

If you buy a paper every day, take a library book for the train in the morning and ask to have someone's paper that they have finished with. Or read papers in the library or online, which are free.

If you continue to buy stuff you don't need, you lock yourself in a prison of despair because you carry all that guilt around with you – and sooner or later, you pay back the money anyway.

This is the beginning of freedom. You are taking control of your life again. It won't take more than a month. Once you have lived on the minimum and repaid what you owe, then you can be easier on yourself.

Think you've got no self-control? Find your willpower. Here's how:

It is somewhere inside you. Here's how to find it. If you like chocolate, buy yourself a small bar. If you prefer something else as a treat, substitute this: biscuits, nuts, smoothies, beer, wine or whatever. Not cigarettes, drugs – and nothing expensive.

Are you back with me? Consume one section of your chosen choccy bar, or take a sip of the beer or whatever. Put the treat away. If necessary, give it to someone else to keep for you. You will have another chocolate later and enjoy it more than the first. You have learned your first lesson in re-orientating your spending.

Now you need to decide on your new cash-crashing budget. You must base this on your new, revised target figures. Take your weekly budget out of the bank. Then you know how much you have and can make the decision to spend no more than that over the course of the week. You could even hide your credit cards or chequebook, or give them to a friend. This concentrates the mind wonderfully. There is simply no room for spending on so much as a bag of peanuts.

Shortcut if you can't be bothered to do the maths
Most people can survive on £50 each a week for everyday expenditure, including food. Some people have to survive on less every week. If you do this, you will probably save hundreds of pounds in a week. I have personally spent under £5 in a week, but that's by growing my own food.

How to stop wasting money on nothing much

Find a small book or old envelope and pencil. Carry it with you and write down everything you spend, immediately you spend it. Total it up. Keep your receipts in the envelope. All of them. You will see how much you have frittered away in the petrol station shop alone. Check handfuls of small change rather than just putting them in your pocket, for rogue coins, etc.

Do not spend anything this month on:

- Clothes

- Shoes

- Anything else you wear or carry or do to yourself for that 'look at me' effect

- Takeaways

- Ready meals from the chiller or frozen cabinet of food shops

- Toys (except if your children have a birthday)

- Tickets to shows (see page 189 for how to have a free night out)

- Videos and DVDs

- CDs and games

- Your collection of anything

- Sports kit

- Gambling

- Drugs and cigarettes if at all possible

- Vitamins unless medically prescribed for you

- Bath or shower gels and toiletries, except basics like toothpaste which I expect you to buy only when you see a two-for-one offer.

Spend a limited sum only on:

- Going out

- Alcohol

- Transport.

> **Top Tip!** Whenever you go out, take only as much cash as you intend to spend.

If you fail one day, tomorrow is another day. Can you cut back and get even the following day? Think how much time you are spending telling yourself off, feeling guilty or concealing what you have done from others. It just isn't worth the emotion and guilt, is it?

At the end of each week, sit down and go over your highs and lows. Begin to recognise areas of weakness or strength.

Remember Paula Radcliffe, the runner tipped for a gold medal who lost confidence and stopped racing suddenly in the Olympics race? That's how crucial the right mindset is.

How to transform your attitude to saving and spending

The two assumptions you need to change

Here are two common ideas which have probably prevented you from saving in the past. Do they lurk somewhere inside you? If so, tell them where to go.

1. An overdraft is a limit, not a target you are supposed to hit each month.

2. A fistful of credit cards does not tell everyone that you are rich and successful, even if they are platinum-plated and studded with diamonds. These simply mean that the companies who issued them are becoming rich at your expense. They could even scream, 'Sucker,' to the outside world, rather than impressing people.

Don't be mean to others. I don't encourage people to be petty in a Scrooge-like way to others. It is not good for anyone's spirit. Stay generous, but if necessary, explain that you are 'doing Jane Furnival's book for a bit' and can't splash out. Hopefully they will buy you a drink.

Don't fritter. For instance, some women buy lipsticks and nail varnish each week as a small treat. Before they can wade through it all – if ever – their mascara and lipsticks will have gone off. They develop a funny smell. The products, I mean, though the women will too, if they use them.

Don't binge. Saving money on one area of life does not mean you have 'extra' to spend elsewhere, if you have debts to pay first. Pay them off.

Don't go shopping as a hobby. Hands up who goes to the shops and DOESN'T come back with more than they intended? Yeah, well. You can go to the naughty step for lying.

Pre-empt the urge to go to the mall. Plan your weekends, evenings and lunchtimes in advance so that you always have something more important to do.

Make concrete arrangements rather than vague promises to yourself. Invite yourself to see friends, offer to walk someone's dog or babysit, go and watch your son play rugby, do the garden or clear out your wardrobe.

- If you need anything, write a list, and give a friend the money to buy the things for you.

- Destroy all credit cards except one to be used for emergency only.

- Avoid discount warehouses or sales.

- Never go shopping in your lunch hour. Window shop only after stores have closed.

- Throw away catalogues within a few minutes of looking at them.

- Don't phone-in catalogue orders.

- Don't internet-shop.

- Don't watch TV shopping channels.

- If you go to see friends, take gifts ready-wrapped. You will get a holiday feeling when shopping outside your normal neighbourhood and be tempted to spend more.

- If you get a sudden urge to shop, call a friend, go swimming, read a magazine, walk in the park, go to the gym or sit in the library.

- If you are tempted to go shopping at a particular time each week, like Saturday morning when you feel vaguely celebratory that you have got through the week, make other arrangements in advance.

Dealing with other people

This is as important as sorting yourself out. 'Peer pressure' doesn't mean being touched up by a lord in the back of a taxi, but an urge we all have to imitate others whom we think of as socially similar to us or just ahead of ourselves in some way – the Joneses who are richer, socially more adept, or whatever.

How many of us have looked at someone else's baby, pet, car or home and thought, 'I'd love one like that'? This impulse is not a bad thing in itself. It is natural and neutral. Like drink, it all depends how you use it.

Explain to your friends and family that you are trying to cut back, or that you're giving this book a try – because you'd be daft if you didn't want to save more money and cut your spending, right?

Don't be too specific about why you are embarking on this plan. Keep your dignity and your financial secrets. I am always amazed at how plain nosey some people can be. If they're real friends, they may invite you over to theirs for a meal or two, saving you money!

Saving money while being surrounded by people who are richer than you

It is tempting to imagine that others are better-off financially than you. But it's probably only your feeling, not reality.

Never try to keep up with your wealthier friends. This is a game you will not win and it is probably how you started running up bills in the first place. You will simply end up with more bills and you will still not feel better-off than them. If they boast about their spending and lifestyle, be pleasant and say, 'Yes, it's a lovely pool/car/boat/helicopter. Thank you so much for inviting us – it's been great.' Again, feel relieved that you don't have to pay for it.

As they say at school during exams, keep your eyes on your own work. Focus on what you are doing for yourself. Other people's lifestyles are not a reflection on you, nor can you measure yourself by what they have. People waste emotion on useless envy. If only they turned that emotion into a determination to do their best for themselves and their families!

If you feel that someone is trying to belittle you and you can't take any more of it, shoot the ground away from under their feet by reverse-boasting about how much you have saved or emphasising what a simple life you lead. 'I try not to go to the shops these days. But I'm very pleased with my charity shop purchase – only 50p.' Very rich people are fascinated by bargains and love saving money. They will immediately want to know your secrets.

Why you should never try to impress people by pretending to have more money than you actually have

Skye worked for a friend of mine, Mary, a fashion P.R. She socialised with a well-off crowd but her salary wouldn't run to new party clothes every week, so instead of investing in charity shop chic, as smart savers would do, Skye took to stealing Mary's clothes samples from her wardrobe. When discovered, she cried and confessed that she had already got deeply into debt, trying to emulate her friends. She swore she would never do it again. Then, when the fuss had died down, Skye stole some jewellery given to Mary by her husband. Ironically, if she had confided in Mary, she would have lent her what she wanted. Skye seemed to want Mary's identity, not just her things.

A flatmate of mine (hello, wherever you are now!) once sold everything he had to the rest of us grubby flatmates, from a jumper to a bicycle, to take a girl out to an expensive lunch. We gathered that he had 'bigged himself up' as my sons would say, in a touching desire to impress this well-off lady! At this lunch, she told him she wasn't interested in seeing him again. Just as well, as I don't know what else he could have sold to take her out again.

Where you live affects your spending and saving

Spending in London, the South East and East of England is higher than for most of the country, but incomes are also higher. Spending in the North East is 17 per cent lower than average. However, this is where the lowest average incomes are recorded, followed by Wales and Northern Ireland.

If you live in the country, expect to spend more than average – £75 on transport, £47 a week on food and non-alcoholic drinks, £63 on recreation and culture and £37 on household goods and services.

The official cost of children

Bringing up a child costs £6,685 each year until the age of 21, according to research by the Liverpool Victoria Friendly Society. In the first five years of their lives, children cost most – £9,339 each year. Childcare for working parents is a great expense, at around £3,217 per year for an under-11.

Having two children runs a coach and horses through your budget. The average weekly expenditure for families with children increases from around £531 for those with one child to £611 for two children, but only to £627 for three or more.

School and university cost £1,646.71 per year up to age 21. Private school fees cost £7,000 on average per year, usually doubled for boarding school and tripled if the boarding school is a bit swish, or caters for special needs. Girls' school fees are slightly cheaper than boys'. A three-year university course costs at least £30,000 with £18,790 for subsistence over and above a student loan. (Source: Prudential.)

> **Top Tip!** Save money by avoiding going to uni in London, which costs up to £2,000 above the average over three years.

Money and the family

Relationships

Money is as important as love and sex in relationships, and causes just as much passion, happiness, chaos and misery. Money means power and control over others. It also means security. It can be a bridge-building tool, a gesture of thanks or of deep caring. It is not the root of all evil, nor something to feel guilty about having. It is neutral. Unlike chocolate, which is entirely a force for good and makes the world go round.

How to say 'no' to those you love

'Saying that you can't afford something, or don't have much money, is like an admission of failure to many people,' says *Christine Northam of Relate*. 'It links into insecurities about the past. People are judgmental and if another person admits they don't have much money, it frightens them by reminding them of their own precarious position. If many people come from less well-off backgrounds, losing money or having less of it leads them to think, "Where do I really belong?"'

Here are some suggestions.

Tell them the truth. Don't lie and don't get over-emotional. Control your tone of voice. 'This has happened. We can't go skiing.'

Don't say a direct 'no'. Try giving them the responsibility of making a choice. 'You can either have an engagement ring, or we have a car. I'm happy either way. You choose.'

Make it a serious occasion. Turn off the TV and sit opposite each other. Have physical bills to hand. Explain, repeatedly if necessary, the financial situation, 'and that is why you cannot have skating shoes/an iPod/a remote-control plane.' Teenagers may need it repeated several times a day.

Try a little-by-little approach. 'I love you but I can't afford it now. Can you think of something else that's a little cheaper and we can go out and get it?'

Don't go back on your refusal. If you refuse to buy one thing and then buy something else later, 'to make up for the disappointment', you have confused the other person and they won't believe you next time.

Children

How to create junior smart savers

'If a stranger knocked on your door and said he wanted to come in and talk to your children, you'd tell him to go away. But that is precisely what is happening to children when they watch television advertisements. It's a huge challenge for parents. There are all these strangers out there who want to get at your children in order to get at you.' *Frank Furedi, Professor of Sociology, University of Kent.*

Parents spend around £715 a year on toys, according to a survey by Egg. That's per child. I hate to think how much parents spend on their own toys.

Children are extremely suggestible, as we know. Teach your children to be critical of what they see and hear. That something available to buy is not always desirable, just because it is on TV or in the newspapers. Let your children hear you discussing adverts. If you can teach your children to look under the surface of the glossy advertising sell, they are on the right track.

Remember to point out that commercial TV, newspapers and magazines make immense sums from advertisers, and that publishing pages of 'new stuff to buy each month' is another form of advertising.

Encourage your children, too, to resist pressure from other children to conform 'because everyone else does or has it'. This takes guts, but you do it by example. I may be a fat old bat but I am not a walking billboard. I wear a dress, not a designer. Nor would I ever wear anything with a label on the outside. My eldest son, when 16, had absorbed these values by silent osmosis.

I bought him a school bag with a certain international sports logo on it, as it was the largest and cheapest I could find. He refused to be seen with it. Why did I expect anything else?!

It is hard, but if kids say that their friends don't want to know them if they don't have certain named products, tell them to get new friends, not new things. Otherwise, there will never be an end to the tunnel of consumerism you enter – and the children you buy these things for will not appreciate your sacrifices to give them the latest trainers or bling. They think it's their 'right'.

'The message children are being given by advertising is that their status is inexorably linked with what they buy and what they wear. It causes a huge amount of conflict and misery. Working parents who feel guilty about not spending time with their children, compensate by buying them what they want. The whole of our society is predicated on buying. There is a huge amount of guilt involved.' *Greg Philo, Professor of Communication at Glasgow University*.

We must not abdicate responsibility for our children's consumerist behaviour. The solution to the problem lies with us. 'Parents can restrict television viewing to half an hour a day or refuse to buy certain foods if they want. Parents need to get back in control and set some boundaries. You don't have to give children television in their bedrooms,' Greg adds.

> **Top Tip!** Don't encourage an obsession with merchandise by kitting out a bedroom in a theme like Spiderman or Barbie. You will have to do it all again when the child moves on to the next obsession.

I suggest paying basic pocket money and top-up sums for special jobs. But don't encourage children to demand payment for things they should do as a matter of course as part of living in a family, like walking the dog, clearing the table, washing up dishes and tidying their rooms. Top-up money is for extra jobs like cleaning the car or mowing the lawn.

I never give my children pocket money unless they ask for it, teaching them a vital lesson for life: If you don't ask, you don't get. I write pocket money in a book which they keep, rather than giving them the sum in cash which they invariably lose. If they want it, I make them ask me for it again and explain why they want it, then we discuss it. It means they have to think how to 'sell' me the idea of making that purchase, rather than buying indiscriminately. The cash book allows them to keep a record of their spending.

I keep money one step back from them because children seem to go through a stage of wanting to buy anything at all, up to the limit of the money they have in their hands, just for the experience of immediate possession. I have seen a child (not mine, fortunately) have a tantrum because they were not allowed to buy slippers they would never wear and were the wrong size but the 'right' price, i.e. all their spending money.

Discuss priorities with children. 'We can have this, or that, but not both.'

Explain that the hole in the wall does not give you any sum of money you want. Most children think it is magical.

> **Top Tip!** If your income is around £30,000 a year or less, your 16–19-year-old who does 12 hours of study at school or a college – even for GCSE retakes – can claim Education Maintenance Allowance (EMA), worth up to £30 a week plus a bonus of up to £500 in two years, and still have a part-time job without affecting your other benefits. For details, try *www.ema.dfes.gov.uk* or call free on 0808 101 6219.

> **Top Tip!** If a child has a tantrum at me in a shop, I have a tantrum back. 'Yes, it's awful, isn't it? I just won't buy it for you,' I wail. That stops them, as they find it embarrassing to be in the shop with you and may resort to dragging you out or offering you a treat like chocolate to shut you up.

Children's savings

You can hold small investments for your children in a simple trust called a 'bare trust' without any expensive legal hoo-hah merely by placing their initials after your name on savings or shares documents. If you think this may be queried, fill out a 'declaration of trust' form which any savings organisation should provide, or add a note to your application form stating that the child is the beneficial owner of the investment.

> **Top Tip!** When children receive money for Christmas or birthdays, take half and put it in a savings account, non-tax-paying of course. They won't notice that you have taken half at the time and will be delighted at this nest-egg on their 18th birthday. Check the columns of weekend money sections in any good newspaper for current best rates.

Children can start having their own building society savings accounts from the age of seven.

Children have personal tax allowances – the amount they can earn before they pay tax – identical to adults (currently £5,225). But if you (the parent) pay money into their savings and it earns over £100 in a year, it is treated as your income, not the child's, and you pay tax on it. If both parents put money in, it can earn £200 before you pay tax. Most unfair.

The solution is that other people, like grand- or godparents, can set up a bare trust for your child in the same simple, child's initials-after-their-name, way. Then the child's own annual personal tax allowance (£5,225) and capital gains tax exemption can both be claimed before tax is paid on the interest earned.

However, the person who generously set up your child's savings must try to live for seven years more, or the child may have to pay inheritance tax on the gift. (This actually happened to my eldest son with my mother, who sadly died a few months short of seven years after giving him a lump sum to pay his school fees. I reflected that he would have been better off if she had given him this money year by year.)

Before a bank or building society will waive tax on the interest paid to a child's account, you generally need to fill out form R85, which they should be able to give you. That's unless the savings account is especially for children, in which case this tax-form stuff should be all done for you.

> **Top Tip!** Moneyfacts, a financial information company, have named the best Children's Account Providers of 2007 as:
> **Winner:** Harpenden Building Society
> **Highly Commended:** Bradford & Bingley
> **Commended:** Furness Building Society.

"

JANE'S GOLDEN TIP
Large sums? Seek legal advice.

"

Trusts normally end when a child reaches 18. But trust law is complex and there are ways of keeping money back from the untrustworthy (pun intended) for longer. With the help of a trust specialist, you can place all sorts of savings inside trusts so that trust fund babes can limit their tax bills in later life. Trust funds to pay private school fees can use a child's tax allowance to stretch the money available.

> **Top Tip!** If you borrow your child's money, do pay interest on it! You are teaching them fair p(l)ay.

National Savings offer Children's Bonus Bonds in £25 units, but uncles and aunties must know the child's saving number before buying, so it's easiest for them to give you the money to buy on their behalf. *www.nsandi.com*, 0845 964 5000.

Individual Savings Accounts (ISAs) are open to teens over 16 and are ways of getting interest without paying tax on it. You can invest £7,000 per tax year: £3,000 in cash, £3,000 in stocks and shares and £1,000 in an insurance ISA. Ask an independent financial advisor, found via IFAP, *www.ifap.org.uk*, 0117 971 1177, or IFAS, *www.aifa.net*, 020 7628 1287.

Friendly Societies take a regular sum and repay the money, usually after ten years or more, tax-free in addition to your ISA tax-free allowance. The rates don't knock my socks off, I have to say. *www.friendlysocieties.co.uk*, 0161 952 5051.

Children born on or after 1 September 2002 receive at least £250 from the state Child Trust Fund, and a further gift on each birthday up till the age of seven. The child can't touch the money until their

18th birthday, but relations and friends can add up to £1,200 a year. An extra £250 is paid to children from families on incomes of £13,500 or less who are eligible for the full Child Tax Credit.

Research suggests that many parents have not placed their child's gift in a savings account yet. For details of special savings accounts for this money, go to *www.childtrustfund.gov.uk*, 0845 302 1470.

> **Top Tips!** Financial Discounts Direct does not offer advice about choosing an ISA, but once you know what you want to buy, may offer discounts you could not get by buying direct. *www.financial-discounts.co.uk*, 01420 549090.

It is worth investing in insurance in case your children have disabling accidents, which will help pay care fees for their lives. It should cost a few pounds. Many private schools offer this, or check with an insurance broker.

Children, money and divorce

Money is power and divorce is the great forum for power fights. A typical problem (there are others, of course) is the father not paying enough child maintenance to the mother, then shelling out eye-watering sums for toys and clothes when seeing the children, to buy their favour. Such people remind me of African dictators who steal their people's financial aid, then drive around throwing money out of their limo windows so they are considered generous.

So try to get the maintenance payments right to begin with. Include an agreement with your ex about treats and shopping, and discuss large gifts with the other parent before bestowing them.

A present is literally this – a way to be 'present' in someone else's life, although you are not physically there. An ex may be giving gifts out of guilt. The most important thing is that the child knows there is no room for manipulation about money and material things, or the sky is the limit.

Bribery doesn't make children love you. It makes them despise you. If you continue to use money to exert power over them as they grow up, they will want the money but they won't want to be controlled by you.

If your ex doesn't believe or appreciate this, show them what I've written here.

The parent support charity Parentline Plus made the point to me that it's important not to get into a competition with your ex about giving the biggest gifts. They said, 'Remember all the things you do give to your children. Don't see your ex's behaviour as an attack on you. It's more about their feelings about the children and themselves as parent than about you. If they have more money, ask if the two of you could work out a way of communicating about what the kids would benefit from and need. After all, there is no point in having lots of expensive toys if what they really need is a new pair of shoes or school uniform.'

Parentline Plus has a free helpline, 0808 800 2222, *www.parentlineplus.org.uk*.

If you have trouble with your ex and money, mediation may be cheaper than going through a solicitor. For more information, see the section on divorce on page 199.

Making older teenagers responsible for their own spending

I am astonished by how some families allow their teenagers to live privileged lives, with their phone bills paid, for instance, while the parents scrimp to save money. If you have the same problem, deal with it as a family by explaining the debt, repeatedly if necessary, and ask them to pay or contribute. Set up a bank or savings account for each teenager and pay into it a budget which has to cover everything, from travel to going out. Help them to budget by making lists.

Make them think about the necessities first – food and travel. Get them an Oyster card if they travel in the London area, to cut their travel costs.

Explain that texting their friends every few minutes is not necessary, and never polite during meals. Suggest that there is a certain romance in not texting all day, but arranging to phone their girl or boyfriend at a certain time and speak to them – remember those sweet conversations that went along the lines of: 'You hang up first.' 'No, you hang up first.'?

Top Tip! Even if they stay out later than agreed, never economise on making sure that they get home safely. Tell them that you will always pay their cab fare home if they find themselves stranded. You can find a way for them to make it up to you, for instance by cleaning your car.

3

Pain-free practical cost-cutting

How to maximise the money that you have and minimize the money that you owe

You could owe a few pounds. Or a fortune. You may want my advice on how to jog along steadily, or to save up for something big like a house deposit. Whatever you need, here are all the options available to you in a Pick-and-Mix format.

Don't go back to bed with your head under the duvet, moaning softly. You won't need to do everything that I suggest here!

> **Top Tip!** Don't keep the odd bill or two a secret, as many people do. You are only cheating yourself, as you will still have to pay.

Make a list of what you owe

Include money borrowed from friends and family members. Taking them for granted can cause family fallings-out – and if nothing else, you want nice presents and a free lunch next Christmas!

To those who would rather drink Baby Bio than make this list. Please put the bottle down. If you poison yourself, your pot plants will have no one to feed them and how could you be so cruel?

Now listen! *Which is worse, nameless fear or the fear you know?* Fear of the unknown is why you don't sleep at nights. You will feel more powerful once you have made this list, because you are taking control.

It's only money. The sun will still shine and small things like your children's smiles will delight you. And with the help I offer you, things will improve. I promise.

Check whether your bills are correct

The first thing to do is get all your nuts and bolts of life tightened! You would be amazed how many everyday bills are wrong. People pay them because they think they are 'official' and who are they to argue? Also, it's really boring to go back over these figures and check them. But set time aside and do it. It's actually terribly pleasurable to find an overpayment.

> **TOP TIP!** Are your gas and electricity bills 'estimated' – with an E before the amount of gas or electricity they claim you have consumed? Well, read the meter and you will probably find that you can reduce those bills. I did – saving several hundred pounds which had clocked up over several years.

My bet is, just by reviewing the various 'payment plans' you are on, you will save yourself hundreds of pounds which you may be pouring away in a year, and gaining nothing in exchange.

It's boring but effective, and at least it means you can save substantial sums without tightening your belt or making sacrifices.

For instance, is your electricity measured on some old payment plan like Economy 7, which is great if you want to run all your appliances in the middle of the night, but not so hot for general all-day consumption? Do you have all your friends and family phone discounts for the phone, or do they need updating? Are you on the right phone tariff? Do you have the cheapest phone supplier? *Don't let these things slide – they are costing you money!*

> **Top Tip!** Companies reduce their prices – they have to remain competitive – but when they introduce new offers they don't tell existing customers. *You have to ask in order to be changed on to these newer and often cheaper options. Now that Virgin has merged with several cable TV and phone companies, I called them and asked, 'Can I have a deal?' I cut over £8 a month from my bill.*

Go through your bank details for direct debit payments

Are there any that you have *forgotten to cancel,* which firms are still collecting, without providing any goods or services in return? I once found one that was two years out of date.

Are there direct debits that you should set up, for instance linked to credit cards you forget to pay? MBNA credit card did not answer the phone for so long and so often that I forgot to set up a direct debit payment to them. The result was a £25 late payment fine and they switched my zero per cent rate to a substantial interest payment, saying that one missed payment negated the zero per cent deal.

Now check direct debits for *poor value*. Payment protection insurance on credit cards or borrowings including a mortgage is one thing to look at. The Citizens Advice Bureau has made a super-complaint to the Office of Fair Trading about this insurance, as the charges can be hefty but only four per cent of customers feel the need to claim, of which a quarter are turned down. (DTI figures).

Cancelling a magazine subscription can typically save £30 a year; gym membership, £600; life insurance, £90; internet connection, £216; club membership, £800.

Check your bank statements

Thirteen per cent of people who check, find a mistake. People think that banks' computers are never wrong, but they can overcharge on everything from ordinary accounts to loans and overdrafts.

If you suspect a mistake and want professional help, either ask your bank to check, which is free, or pay an accountant, or for larger sums, try John Moran of BCALC Associates Ltd, *www.bankaudits.co.uk*, 01372 479799, who for a fee of around £350 plus 25 per cent of the sum recovered, will do the spadework for you. If he finds no error, he returns the fee. He says he has never had to return a fee.

You may also be entitled to refunds on things like insurance if you have prepaid then stopped the policy halfway through the year, but you have to keep a close check and hassle. For instance, when my mother died, the TV licensing people – renowned for this – kept sending her bills, then rude letters refusing to believe that she was dead. After the umpteenth time, I spoke to someone there who saw sense and informed me that I should have claimed a large refund on her estate's behalf.

Some people are reclaiming hundreds or even thousands from their banks – the allegedly over-high charges the banks have made them pay for up to six years previously, for overdrafts and cashing cheques when they have gone overdrawn. Many banks have refunded money, but there are signs that they are becoming tougher, and some retaliate by threatening to close the accounts of anyone who reclaims money – so make sure you have a Plan B bank lined up before starting this process.

You do not need to pay any company to reclaim your bank charges on your behalf. You can get detailed instructions about how to do it for yourself, including the wording of letters, from websites such as *www.thisismoney.co.uk/bankcharges*. You can also get copies of all your statements six years back for no more than £10 if you ask your bank for a printout, rather than the more expensive statement on the bank's best headed paper.

If you have other bank and credit card refund complaints, *www.bankcomplaints.co.uk*, 01752 294205, can reclaim charges on your behalf on a no-win, no-fee basis.

Can't stand opening your letters because of the bills?

Get someone else to do it. It may be better than you thought. When my father died, we thought he had no money. I steeled myself to open a pile of old letters and found they contained several cheques.

Don't bottle up the stress. If you become depressed, nothing will get paid and things will never improve. Talk to someone. If not a friend or member of your family, try a professional from one of the debt counselling charities listed here. They have heard it all before and aim to get you out of trouble. No one is going to tell you off. What is done, is done.

> **Top Tip!** Don't lie in bed letting it all go to your head. Get the back of an envelope – don't waste good money on notepads! – and jot it down.
> In the morning things will look better and you automatically feel more in control when you are standing up, rather than lying down.

Hold a family meeting so everyone knows it's important

Find a time when even teenagers can make it, and allow over an hour. Turn off the TV and phones. Have this book to hand and work through this list. Put everyone in the picture of how serious the problem is and ask them to give up one thing. Try not to argue.

Don't waste time in recriminations. We are now problem-solving. Just plod on. Tell everyone in advance that if anyone storms off, a decision will be made and enforced by the remaining members about how the stormer-outer can cut down their spending – for instance, all surplus DVDs and games will be sold – so if they prefer to have control, they had better stay. Ask everyone to think what they can give up and what other people in the group can give up. If they don't want it to be personal, they can write suggestions down and put it in a hat to be read out by the chairman of the meeting.

Work out whether this is a one-off situation or a long-term problem. An unexpected dental or vet bill, or a sudden demand for money for a school holiday can strain a budget that's already on a knife-edge. Debt advisors say that one of the biggest causes of running up debts is your overtime suddenly drying up, so if this has happened, read my section on making extra money or make a cunning plan.

Think big

You may decide to make sweeping changes to your life to improve your financial situation. It can be easier and more effective to do one big thing, like moving house, and save a lot at a stroke, than to do loads of little things.

"

JANE'S GOLDEN TIP

If you have set your heart on a particular state school, move to a house outside the gates. Or become the caretaker and live in a little house just inside the gates. State school waiting lists don't give priority to your children according to how long you have waited, but by considerations like siblings in the school and how close you live – so you can wait for a year and still find your place taken by someone who moved in yesterday. Also, don't believe estate agents who say a particular house is in a school's catchment area. Phone the school and check, then check again before exchanging contracts on your new home. Some catchment areas change annually depending on the number of applications and siblings.

"

Now we have dealt with the basics, let's see if we can make your existing income magically expand. Check whether you're making the most of your income here.

Making ends meet

Are you owed money? It always astonishes me how few companies know that you can claim huge sums in interest from them, if they don't pay up in time. Under the Late Payment of Commercial Debts (Interest) Act 1998, if you are self-employed and have money overdue from a business, after 30 days of non-payment, you can charge a substantial one-off penalty sum (which varies with how much is owed) plus interest on the debt at eight per cent above the Bank of England interest rate in the January or June closest to your invoice date, making at the time of writing, 13.5 per cent. The business that owes you money is not allowed to dictate its payment terms to you without your prior agreement, so it can't say: 'Not paying you for a year is our standard business practice so take it or leave it.' A gentle reminder of the legal position may work wonders.

Top Tip! Send regular updates with the penalties and interest sums added. If the people who owe you money want to negotiate, you can offer to reduce the interest. For more information and a calculator, see *www.late-payment-law.co.uk*.

"

JANE'S GOLDEN TIP
Join a union. If you have any trouble like not being paid, its free legal advice, personal support and extras like insurance cover are

> *more than worth the subscription, which is tax-deductible if you are self-employed.* **"**

If the debt is personal, you can take someone to court at the Small Claims Court. I have done this successfully, though it was stressful and time-consuming, not least for the three good friends who took time off work to support me and give evidence. I was awarded a good rate of interest on what I was owed and my court costs of around £230, and was 'lucky' enough to be paid by my opponent, a store which had not delivered the goods I paid for. (See below.)

You can start proceedings over the internet at *www.moneyclaim.gov.uk* but if you can't resolve your case before going to court, check with your local court on the cost of court fees on top of the initial payment. If you win, it may be hard to get your money if the other person is an experienced dodger or just plain hard-up.

"

JANE'S GOLDEN TIP

Be prepared for your opponent to allege that you behaved so appallingly that you don't deserve to be paid. This is my experience and that of every single person I know who has been to court.

"

MY GOLDEN TIP FOR LIFE *People who behave badly will go on to behave worse. Only in stories do they reform.*

Tax

I am told that the Inland Revenue aims to get only three out of four tax calculations right. Check your bill before paying.

If you are an employee, rather than self-employed, Instant Tax Refund's software can help you reduce tax and claim obscure allowances, backdated for up to six years, as long as you have worked from home at least one day a week, with no complicated forms to complete. If successful, the company claims it can help you save an average of £400. The software package costs £29.95 from 0800 064 0270 or *www.instanttaxrefund.co.uk*.

Is your tax code right? Don't assume the tax people are always right. For more information, try *www.taxcredits. inlandrevenue.gov.uk*. Ask the Inland Revenue, 0845 300 3900 (UK); 0845 603 2000 (Northern Ireland). Or contact an accountant.

Refunds Direct, 0800 1077 188, *www.refundsdirect. co.uk*, has a one-minute questionnaire you can fill out and submit online to discover whether they can help you make savings. They currently claim that the average refund is £800.

The website *www.msn.co.uk* has a useful tax calculator.

If you earn over £5,200 p.a. you pay National Insurance.

If you are contracted-in to the state pension scheme, you pay 11 per cent on weekly earnings between £101 and £670 and one per cent on all earnings above that.

If contracted-out, you pay 9.4 per cent plus one per cent on earnings over £670. Find out if you are contracted in or out by asking your employer or tax office. For more advice, seek an independent financial adviser.

It is worth running your tax bill past an accountant or tax adviser, even if you are employed and it is all done for you at work. Tax experts know the latest ways to avoid tax and will aim to save you money, their fee at least.

Saving on your tax bill if you're self-employed

The way to save most on tax is to go self-employed and/or form a limited company. Consult an accountant first. Self-employed National Insurance rates start at £2.20 a week on earnings of £4,635 p.a., rising to eight per cent on profits between £5,225 and £34,840 and one per cent after that. To avoid paying National Insurance, pay yourself a low income and take dividends on your company shares instead; but this may be challenged in the courts in the future, so read the papers.

Being self-employed involves saving all your till receipts and bills. Before you calculate your 'taxable income', you may claim expenses on everything from using your home, phone and car to newspapers and accountancy advice. Claim enough expenses and your taxable income dips so low that you pay a fraction of the tax which an employee on a similar income would pay. If you register for VAT, you reclaim this on office equipment etc. too. On the other hand, by going self-employed, you lose holiday and sick pay, entitlement to benefits and other safety nets. You must keep proper accounts. Several people I know have not, and thought they were very clever until it emerged that they could not get a mortgage.

One of the biggest savings is claiming, as a tax-deductible expense, the use of part of your home as an office, including utility bills. But to avoid paying capital gains tax when you sell your home, be hazy about which room it is. Make sure you put a sofa-bed, a box of Christmas decorations, or anything not connected with the business into the room too.

To calculate the cost of a home office, work out how many rooms you have, excluding kitchen, bathrooms and hall, then add together annual costs of utilities, council tax and insurance (both buildings and contents). Divide by the number of eligible rooms. Fifty per cent of this sum is the amount you can offset against tax.

How employed people can save tax

Do not assume that 'they' work out your tax and National Insurance correctly. Mistakes can go on for years. If you are employed, check your tax code. The usual code is 522L. If you have an 'x' or 'month 1' written after your code, you may be on emergency tax rates, which can be higher. Phone the Inland Revenue tax helpline and ask why.

Tax benefits you can get from your employer (if only anyone knew ...)

Bicycles. The Cycle to Work Initiative saves employees 40–50 per cent of the total cost of a bicycle and accessories. The company buys the bicycle for you and then leases it on to you, usually for 18 months. When the lease ends, you buy the bicycle for about the cost of one month's lease. You don't pay VAT on the bike, and as the repayments are taken out of your gross monthly salary (i.e. before tax), you save 22 per cent in income tax and 11 per cent on National Insurance contributions for that sum.

Free meals and drinks. As a further perk, employers may provide free meals and drinks to employees who cycle to work. As long as the benefit is provided on a specially designated cycle-to-work day, meals provided as an incentive to employees who get on their bikes are free of tax. Employers can offer these days as many times as they like. Every day if they want.

Travel expenses. People who travel by car for business – other than to the office – should keep a mileage log. If your employer does not reimburse the costs, you can claim these off your tax bill. 40p per mile for the first 10,000 miles and 25p per mile after that.

Uniform. Wear a tee-shirt with the firm's logo on it to work. (It can't just be a pin-on badge.) Then you can try claiming up to £60 a year off your tax bill for laundering a 'uniform'.

Childcare. Up to £55 weekly in Childcare Vouchers is exempt from tax and NI. Although there is a service charge, they actually cost less than giving cash.

Mobile phones. The employer provides a phone for the employee and pays his mobile phone bills, taking the cost back from your earnings before tax and NI, which both employer and employee save paying. You do not have to use the phone for work. Where more than one phone is provided, some costs may be liable for tax.

Financial planning. Employers can provide financial information and advice up to a value of £150 per worker, without landing the employee with a tax bill.

Season tickets. Here the employer will lend you the money you need to buy an annual season ticket, interest-free. You pay the money back each month via a deduction in your salary. There is no tax charge provided the loan is less than £5,000.

Boosting your income

Is everyone in your house contributing to bills? I have helped families simply by telling them to charge their grown-up children some rent and living expenses.

'The way you're living in your grandmother's flat rent-free is like climbing on her back and asking her to carry you,' I told one young lady who, at 22, was old enough to know better. She was upset at the time, but a week later the message had sunk in and she thanked me for pointing this out. She started paying rent, and said she felt better because of it. Her grandmother could then afford a few little extras, which was great as, before then, she sat in the local launderette to keep warm.

Under the Inland Revenue's Rent-a-Room scheme, if you have a door between you and a lodger, even if that is your teenager and/or the door is locked all the time, you can charge £4,250 in rent tax-free each year, split between couples if the house is jointly owned. This also applies, apparently, if you rent out your home for a couple of weeks a year while you are not there. You have to declare this income on your tax return.

> **Top Tip!** If you have family members who want to go to college, seek extra funding through scholarships offered by colleges and by outside businesses and organisations. For instance, the Army offers financial help to people who pledge to join them afterwards. There are also engineering scholarships and advertising scholarships. For help and information, try *www.scholarship-search.org, www.hotcourses.com/studentmoney,* or *www.educationuk.org/scholarships.* Your library might stock the *Educational Grants Directory,*

The Grants Register, or *The Charities Digest*, which list thousands of wonderful small charities with sums of money, perhaps left long ago by benevolent old buffers, to educate the daughters of clergymen in the West Riding of Yorkshire, or the sons of miners in the Rhondda Valley, and similar. The Educational Grants Advisory Service tel: 020 7254 6251 will search through them for you to identify which you might be eligible for.

Insurance. If you owe money because you are sick or have lost your job, check with your credit card companies in case you are covered by Payment Protection Insurance. Check your insurance policies in case there is any help lurking in the small print.

Unlocking part of your pension. If you are over fifty, you may be able to get hold of part of your pension fund as a tax-free lump sum. Check with your pension provider.

Benefits. £4.5 billion goes unclaimed every year, because people don't know they're entitled to it. Don't be shy. Any household earning up to £58,000 per year or £66,000 if you have a child under one, is entitled to children's Tax Credits – not actually a credit, but a sum of money paid to you weekly. If you earn under £16,000 a year, even if you're self-employed, you can claim Tax Credits too. If your income is borderline, remember to claim pension contributions and charitable donations off that income to qualify for the benefit.

There are some benefits for everyone, whatever your income or savings. I have lost count of the number of people over 65 and in need of personal care that I have advised to claim an Attendance Allowance – a sum of either £43.15 or £64.50 to pay for personal care at home. 0800 88 22 00, *www.directgov.uk* or type 'attendance allowance' into your computer search engine to download a form. This allowance is not means-tested, meaning that you don't have to state your income or savings. The Benefits Office or Citizens Advice Bureau can help you fill in the form if you ask. The benefit is paid from the day you ask for the form – so do it today!

"

JANE'S GOLDEN TIP

Fill in any official application form as fully as you can. Leave no space blank, even if you write 'not applicable' or put a line through it. Otherwise you face delays.

"

Then there is the Nursery Education Grant, which you have to ask a nursery to claim for you. That covers up to two-and-a-half hours a day of free nursery care for pre-school children. For information, ask the Maternity Alliance, 0207 490 7638.

The Community Legal Service Direct, *www.clsdirect. org.uk*, 0845 345 4345, gives clear advice on all benefits available. Or contact your council's Welfare Rights Office or a local (free) Law Centre, listed in your phone directory or via *www.lawcentres.co.uk* or the Law Centres Federation, 020 7387 8570. A second website, *www.lawcentres.org*, has useful links to other specialised helplines to advise on benefits for specific groups like the disabled. Finally, you can contact *www.adviceguide.org.uk*, the website of the Citizens Advice Bureau, whose local branch will be listed in your library.

British Gas Warm-a-life is a scheme offering benefit checks and free energy-saving tips to people living in privately owned or privately rented houses who receive income-related benefits (not just British Gas customers). Call 0845 605 2535, and go for option 4, 'quality of life'.

If you are over 60, check what you are entitled to by contacting Age Concern's information line: 0800 00 99 66, *www.ageconcern.org.uk*. Or try Help the Aged's Seniorline: 0808 800 6565 (0808 808 7575 Northern Ireland) and The Pension Service, *www.thepensionservice.gov.uk*, 0845 60 60 265.

Rebates. Are you sick or disabled? Or if you have a low income, perhaps you can claim a rebate on your rent and council tax.

Charity funds and grants. Contact your workplace or industry union, even if you are not a member. Some have hardship funds and can pay to support people who have suddenly fallen on hard times.

There are also substantial charity funds to help people, some set up centuries ago and under-used because no one knows about them. Consider your present or former work, and also family connections with specific types of work. If you have ever worked in the theatre – even selling ice-creams – or on newspapers, for instance, or as a travelling salesperson, you may be able to get crisis payments.

You can check for relevant charities in The Charities Digest 2007, £34.50 plus £2.95 p&p, published by Waterlow Professional Publishing (*www.waterlowlegal.com*, Waterlow Professional Publishing, Paulton House, 8 Shepherdess Walk, London N1 7LB) – but save money and order it from your library or check in your local reference library. You never know what you can get until you try.

Take on a second job. Gain extra income from occasional work or make the best use of what you already have, without setting up a business or working full-time. See my chapter on ways of making extra money without getting a regular job (page 103).

Sell something. See page 89.

Remember forgotten savings. Go through old files and check whether policies are worth anything, or if old building society accounts are dead or just dormant. By doing this, at a time of crisis, I discovered a life policy worth over £2,000 that saved my bacon at one stage. The Unclaimed Assets Register can help you track down old savings policies. 0870 241 1713, *www.uar.co.uk*.

JANE'S GOLDEN TIP

While we are talking about forgotten money, check your fruit dish, down the side of the sofa and even old envelopes for cash stashes that come in handy. I recently found a £50 note in an envelope I was about to throw away, and was happy for a week.

Restructure your financial arrangements

Here's how to make your existing income go further.

Ruthlessly renegotiate your mortgage

It is said that we waste up to £1,200 each year because we don't switch to better deals. If you pay a standard variable rate, I suggest making it a priority to find something lower. Saving even one per cent of a £90,000 mortgage over 25 years can net you £22,500, according to *www.debtfreeday.com.*

The bean-counters among us get very worked up about making sure mortgages are the first things to be paid off, but, I have to say, I don't think this strategy is right for everyone.

I actually don't think that paying off your mortgage quickly is a social or financial necessity, if it makes you live uncomfortably. I have done it once and it didn't make me feel I had achieved a great life goal, though my husband disagrees.

Here's my view and it's controversial. Life can be short and uncertain. Make sure you buy a saleable house that you enjoy living in, in as good an area as you can. Don't deceive yourself on this and don't tell yourself your house is worth a lot more than it is. (I confess, I've done this before now.) If you plan on selling your family home and can bear to downsize when the family moves out, and IF house prices in your area go on rising, I hope you could pay off your mortgage from the profits of its sale.

By flogging yourself now to pay off that mortgage extra fast, you are just giving yourself a needlessly hard time. Going without family holidays, for example, to pay off the mortgage a month or two earlier is all very well until you realise that your family has now grown up and gone, leaving you sitting in a paid-for pile of nice bricks but wishing you'd done more with the kids when they were younger. I am not advocating spending all your money on luxury holidays but simply achieving a balance.

If you pay off your mortgage before you die, your children may end up paying inheritance tax on the value of the house. But if you don't and the rest of your mortgage is subtracted from the house value after your death, that may push the value of your estate underneath the inheritance tax threshold, saving shedloads of money.

The websites *www.landsearch.net* or *www.ourproperty.co.uk* will tell you how much houses really sold for, rather than estate agents' headline prices.

Before starting to renegotiate your mortgage, check what rate you are paying, and whether it will change shortly – if you are about to come out of a special deal, for instance.

Check that your mortgage provider won't charge you a penalty to leave them. But even if they do, it may be worth paying it for a better deal. Also, check a potential new lender's arrangement charges, plus legal and valuation costs which can make the cost several thousand pounds higher. That means that a saving of £25 a month on a slightly better interest rate won't be worth moving for.

To find better deals, you can use internet sites like *www.thisismoney.co.uk* or check the 'best mortgage' columns in the money pages of the Saturday papers, but personally I prefer using an independent mortgage broker. They often have more muscle to wrestle the best deals from mortgage providers and justify their fees, which should be stated transparently to you. *These are not the same as independent financial advisers, who often then use mortgage brokers as part of their team.*

For example, mortgage brokers London & Country claim to have 'exclusive deals not available elsewhere'. 0800 953 0304, *www.lcplc.co.uk.*

To compare offers, ask for the total cost of the mortgage over two years, including repayments, fees and your exit penalties from your present mortgage provider. You can use a mortgage calculator on any money site to work out your payments. There is one at *www.msn.co.uk*. Personally, I should make the provider sweat for your business by making them do the maths for you. (Money websites also have calculators for stamp duty, endowment policies and virtually every other financial product you own.)

Top Tip! So many silly savers simply assume all banks and building societies offer broadly similar rates, and just ask their local or normal branch for a mortgage or loan. This is either lazy or crazy. However, if you can't be bothered to do the rounds and just because I love you so much, a company called Moneyfacts names the five cheapest mortgage providers at the time of writing (at standard rates and omitting special deals) as: ING Direct (UK), Stafford Railway Building Society, Harpenden Building Society, The One Account and Newbury Building Society. This goes to show that rather than sticking to big TV-advertised names, the smaller building societies are worth considering. Even if you live nowhere near them.

"

JANE'S GOLDEN TIP

As a handy guide to every good financial deal out there, here are the 2007 award-winners from financial information people Moneyfacts. I can't claim that in each case

their products are best for you personally.
However, just as wise people eating out in
a foreign country choose the restaurant the
locals dine at, it is always worth seeing what
financial industry insiders rate as best.
If you want a shortcut or a reasonable deal,
start with these.

"

Moneyfacts Awards 2007 Winners

Best Fixed Rate Mortgage Provider (without redemption tie-in) – 2 years

Winner: Portman Building Society
Highly Commended: Alliance & Leicester
Commended: Yorkshire Building Society

Best Fixed Rate Mortgage Provider (with extended redemption tie-ins)

Winner: West Bromwich Building Society
Highly Commended: Derbyshire Building Society
Commended: Market Harborough Building Society

Best Fixed Rate Mortgage Provider (without redemption tie-in) – 3 years

Winner: Britannia Building Society
Highly Commended: Portman Building Society
Commended: Yorkshire Building Society

Best Variable Rate Mortgage Provider

Winner: Chesham Building Society

Highly Commended: Yorkshire Building Society
Commended: Hinckley & Rugby Building Society

Best Fixed Rate Mortgage Provider (without redemption tie-ins) – 5 years and over

Winner: Yorkshire Building Society
Highly Commended: Newcastle Building Society
Commended: Leeds Building Society

Best Discounted Rate Mortgage Provider

Winner: Nottingham Building Society
Highly Commended: Alliance & Leicester
Commended: Dunfermline Building Society

Best Remortgage Provider

Winner: Direct Line
Highly Commended: Alliance & Leicester
Commended: Nationwide Building Society

Best Self-Certification Mortgage Provider (NOTE FROM JANE – this is for people who can't provide evidence of their income.)

Winner: Standard Life Bank
Highly Commended: Bristol & West Mortgages
Commended: UCB Home Loans

Best Flexible Mortgage Provider

Winner: Woolwich
Highly Commended: Coventry Building Society
Commended: Hinckley & Rugby Building Society

Best 100% Mortgage Provider

Winner: Co-operative Bank

Highly Commended: Yorkshire Building Society

Commended: Cheshire Building Society

Best Current Account and Offset Mortgage Provider

Winner: The One account

Highly Commended: Intelligent Finance

Commended: Woolwich

Best Current Account Provider (credit interest)

Winner: Alliance & Leicester

High Commended: Nationwide Building Society

Commended: Lloyds TSB

Best Current Account Provider (debit interest)

Winner: Alliance & Leicester

Highly Commended: Nationwide Building Society

Commended: Intelligent Finance

Best Credit Card Provider (introductory rate)

Winner: Sainsbury's Bank

Highly Commended: Sky

Commended: Nationwide Building Society

Best Card Provider (standard rate)

Winner: Intelligent Finance

Highly Commended: Co-operative Bank

Commended: Yorkshire Building Society

Best Credit Card Provider (balance transfer rate)

Winner: Halifax
Highly Commended: Sky
Commended: HSBC

Best No Notice Account Provider

Winner: Anglo Irish Bank
Highly Commended: Chelsea Building Society
Commended: Skipton Building Society

Best internet-only Account Provider

Winner: Bradford & Bingley
Highly Commended: Sainsbury's Bank
Commended: Leeds Building Society

Best Notice Account Provider

Winner: Anglo Irish Bank
Highly Commended: Tipton & Coseley Building Society
Commended: Scottish Widows Bank

Best Monthly Interest Account Provider

Winner: Bradford & Bingley
Highly Commended: Chelsea Building Society
Commended: First Direct

Best Regular Savings Account (variable rate)

Winner: Scarborough Building Society
Highly Commended: Bath Building Society
Commended: Monmouthshire Building Society

JANE'S GOLDEN TIP

"

When you call your mortgage provider and announce that you intend to switch, add enough detail to convince them that you are serious. Tell them the name of your new mortgage provider and the rate they offer. They will almost certainly put you through to a special branch of customer services with orders to offer you their best secret/cheap 'discounted rate' deals to persuade you to stay.

"

They won't show all their cards at once. They may start by matching the deal you have found. This is the point at which you play mortgage providers off against each other in a bid to get them to add extra freebies like flexible terms, payment holidays, waived fees, survey fees and legal fees if any. *Don't agree to any deal without going back to the other side to see if they can better the offer.*

Why does it happen? These days, staff at financial institutions are under tremendous pressure to sell their products to customers. I have heard of senior managers with thirty years' experience being told off for not reaching marketing departments' dreamed-up targets. One financial friend of mine left his work because he could no longer offer clients a normal service, he said.

Invent a 'her indoors' or equivalent whom you 'have to' consult before agreeing to any offer. When trying to decide whether to take an offer or not, buy time by acting helpless. 'I really don't know what to say about your kind offer of a reduced interest rate/free fitted kitchen/crate of wine/woolly hat with your logo on it. I'll have to ask my husband/friend/ the other mortgage company/accountant/penfriend in Kiev/pet Siamese/Oracle and come back to you.' Keeping companies waiting before you take up an offer tends to extract the last possible ounce of lowered interest rates from them as further inducements to you.

Also check offset mortgages which combine your mortgage with your savings and current account, and perhaps your loan and credit card balances. When your salary is paid into it, this kind of account reduces your mortgage and interest, if only for a few days. Offset mortgages can save money long term, but tend to charge higher interest rates.

Check whether your mortgage interest is calculated daily. Daily interest calculations save you thousands.

Consider tracker mortgages which automatically vary interest according to Bank of England base rate. If this falls, the rates adjust immediately. I have heard people complain that with ordinary mortgages it takes several months for rates to adjust in line with interest-rate changes.

> **Top Tip!** If you are locked into an annual mortgage deal and you repay a large sum into it, phone the mortgage provider and ask for the date when the interest is calculated. Repay in time to meet that date and no sooner. Meanwhile, put that sum into an interest-paying ISA account. Otherwise, the money may simply sit there doing nothing.

If you want to pay debts off, put mortgages with cashback on your 'Things to check out' list. These give you an upfront sum. That doesn't mean it is free, though. There is no such thing as a free lunch.

You can also consider interest-only mortgages. These give you a reduced payment. But they do nothing to pay back the original house loan. At the end of that time, you have to repay the original price of the house, either through savings you have prepared or by simply selling the house. This assumes that house prices go up and you will make a profit, though it may not be large enough to buy you another house or see you through retirement. Consider – but treat with great caution.

Putting credit card debt onto your mortgage gives you an interest rate that is much lower than credit card charges, although you will be paying it off for years and it is ultimately more expensive than a short, sharp repayment straight back to the card companies. Keep putting debt onto your mortgage and you could lose your home.

> **Top Tip!** Keep your original mortgage document carefully. Anyone paying off their mortgage, who in the last six years has been charged more in 'exit fees' than the mortgage document stated, is entitled to a full refund. If you feel you have been unfairly charged in any way, contact your mortgage provider and tell them so. You may be surprised by what they will offer.

Look again at your home and buildings insurance. Don't automatically buy it through your mortgage provider and don't assume you have to have contents and buildings insured with the same company. I always think it pays to go to an independent insurance broker. They will want your business and will do all that boring phoning around to get you a better deal. A broker need not live near you as you will probably never meet. Find one via BIBA, the British Insurance Brokers' Association, 0901 814 0015, *www.biba.org.uk*. There are also websites that will do all the legwork, so you only have to fill in one online form to receive quotes from many of the biggest insurance houses. *www.confused.com* is very efficient.

"

JANE'S GOLDEN TIP

If your house is worth more than £300,000 (at rebuilding cost), and/or your contents over £50,000, a high-net-worth insurance company may prove a better deal and may actually be

*around two per cent cheaper than a High
Street standard insurance policy. They work
on the principle that better-off people look
after their things more carefully, i.e. have
burglar alarms, house sitters etc., and are
not such a poor general risk. These high-net-
worth insurers tend to offer more benefits,
like new-for-old cover rather than marking
down the value of items for depreciation,
home business cover, cover for outbuildings,
free fire checks, and a more personal service.
High-net-worth insurers include Chubb, Axa,
Hiscox, and Norwich Union's Tapestry Policy.
It is worth getting quotes from all, or saving
time and trouble by getting a broker to do
it. The Country Gentlemen's Association will
tailor-make the best quote for you from a
selection of high-net-worth insurers. And
real people answer the phone and talk in a
friendly, personal, intelligent way. For free.
You don't have to be a member. 01985
850706, www.thecga.co.uk.*

"

**Things you can do to lower your insurance bill,
without changing insurer.**

Check whether you are in a Neighbourhood Watch
area (or start one yourself if you are not, via the
police).

Install mortice door and window locks – check which
are specified first, with your insurer.

Also check with your insurer before installing a serviced alarm. An approved brand should reduce your premiums.

> **Top Tip!** Before buying a serviced alarm, check whether the system makes regular premium rate calls to check the line early in the morning every day. Some companies can cost you several pounds a week by setting their equipment to do this. I soon found out that the ADT alarm in my new home was doing this and reclaimed the cost from the company in the form of a bottle of wine – before changing to a different company.

Renegotiate your basic utility bills

It takes about six weeks and doesn't involve relaying pipes or cables to switch gas, electricity, water, TV and phone providers. You can save hundreds. The comparison service Simply Switch, *www.simplyswitch. co.uk*, 08000 111 395, claims that you can cut your phone bill by up to 70 per cent by switching phone suppliers, for instance.

Unfortunately, at the time of writing, green power suppliers were not the cheapest.

Check that the websites you use have signed up to the Energywatch Confidence Code, a new system to ensure that they give you impartial information. Energywatch is a consumer watchdog. *www.*

energywatch.org.uk, 0845 906 0708. Websites that have been accredited include:

- *www.energylinx.co.uk*
- *www.simplyswitch.com*
- *www.saveonyourbills.co.uk*
- *www.homeadvisoryservice.com*
- *www.ukpower.co.uk*
- *www.unravelit.com*
- *www.moneysupermarket.com*
- *www.theenergyshop.com*
- *www.which.co.uk/switch*
- *www.uswitch.com*.

Before starting to assemble your latest bills, ask suppliers if they charge different rates at different times of the day and whether there are any penalties for ending a fixed contract, or deals for supplying both gas and electricity.

Ofgem, *www.ofgem.gov.uk*, 020 7901 7295 has a full list of licensed energy suppliers.

> **Top Tip!** Check whether a comparison service has a Code of Conduct or similar. Some comparison services don't carry all the options because they take commission payments from energy suppliers to be listed. It is worth getting feedback from a few comparison services before settling on one.

www.energyhelpline.com, 0800 074 0745, may offer you £20 cashback to make a switch or refer someone. *www.switchandgive.com* offers a donation to charity for a switch. Other services include *www.uswitch. com*, 0845 601 2856, *www.loot.com* (telephone details for your local office listed on the website and in the magazine) and *www.switchwithwhich.co.uk*, 0800 533 031.

If you have a large home, or a large bill, consider switching to a business energy tariff. You can save up to 40 per cent off your domestic bill, but you may have to pay full VAT rather than the reduced VAT for domestic gas and electricity, plus various government fuel taxes. Get your calculator out as I have found comparison services don't do all the sums for you. Two typical comparison services are *www.businessutilities. co.uk*, 0800 619 1270, and *www.ukpower.co.uk*.

> **Top Tip!** Once you have changed suppliers, you can add the cherry to the icing on the cake by adding additional discounts for paying via the internet, direct debit etc., not to mention gaining bonuses such as Nectar points offered by EDF Energy.

If you have a low income, you probably pay more for your fuel because you can't take up discount offers for direct debits. Check the rates offered by EquiGas and EquiPower, non-profit-making companies offering gas and electricity to all customers at one rate. *www.ebico.co.uk*, 0845 458 7689.

JANE'S GOLDEN TIP

If anyone messes up the transfer of power, extract extra credit from them, normally in £20 chunks for the inconvenience.

> **Top Tip!** Get your boiler fixed or replaced in summer, when it is much cheaper.

Saving money on broadband connections

Costs have decreased to as little as £9.99 per month at time of writing. But many broadband providers lock you into a year's contract, so don't waste your time shopping around until you are free of any existing contracts. Use a comparison service like *www.buy3cows.com* to find a better deal.

A TV-plus-broadband war has broken out between BSkyB, BTVision and NTL. All will be offering 'bundles' with combinations of mobile or landline telephone, TV and broadband. Other 'bundling' deals include Tiscali, TalkTalk, Virgin.net and Orange. Some offer cheap or free broadband with mobile telephone contracts. BT will combine it with Freeview, via a set-top box. Sometime this year, Tiscali is promising customers free phone rental and calls for £19.99 a month, with broadband. They claim a saving of £220 a year compared with BT.

> **Top Tip!** If you live in the country, you can pay up to 240 per cent more than others for the same broadband service now that TalkTalk, Sky,

UK Online, Virgin Media, AOL and Tiscali are, it seems, introducing two-tier pricing. It is worth switching by using a comparison service like *www.uSwitch.com* which searches for the best deal based on your postcode.

Be careful of any offer if you pay BT for your line rental and check whether you still have to pay this on top of your new deal.

Here are the questions to ask:

1. Is there an extra set-up fee?

2. Do they provide an engineer to come and get you started, or do they simply send the kit and instructions in a box? Getting started, especially if you are not IT-literate and have an Apple Mac, can be tricky, in my opinion. Treat telesales-people's assurances with sceptism – you'll never find them again to wring their necks when it goes wrong.

3. Would you be on a time limit or a maximum-download limit which might drive a coach-and-horses through your plans to download music or upload photographs? (1GB equals 205 music tracks or 10,500 web pages per month).

4. What is the speed of connection? 1 Mb is around twice as fast as the cheaper 512Kb service, though the latter is adequate for browsing rather than downloading music or film clips.

The switch to a new broadband provider should take about 20 minutes. But if you work from home and rely on broadband to do your job, be wary of changing. I have received consumer complaints, hoping I would help, that the old broadband service stays 'camped' on your phone line, stopping the new one from taking over – and some people have ended up paying for both. Use only Internet Service Providers (ISPs) who have signed up to the Ofcom code of practice, and who give you a migration authorisation code (MAC) within five days of your request to transfer.

Switching to a cable broadband can be even more problematic as you need the new line installed before switching your phone line, and again you can end up paying for both. If you encounter problems try the Internet Service Providers' Association, *www.ispa. org.uk*, 0870 0500 710.

Phone using your broadband. Save money on phone line rental and call costs by connecting a modem to your PC and phoning for nothing via your broad band connection. You can use the computer at the same time. The snag is, calls inward to you cost more: BT tells me 5p a minute as opposed to the usual 3p-ish.

Top Tip! You no longer have to pay BT for your phone line rental – the factor that pushed up the price of switching phone providers. TalkTalk OneTel guarantees lower rentals than BT together. 0800 957 0178, *www.talktalk.co.uk*.

Replace your satellite or cable TV

Here are the main options:

FreeView. This has nothing really to do with free satellite channels and gives you access to digital terrestrial TV – around 30 channels including BBC3 and 4, ITV2, CBeebies and UKTV History. To get this, you buy a decoder box for around £40 and pay nothing more or buy a new TV with the service built-in. *www.freeview.co.uk* will tell you whether you are in the right area to receive the service. 08701 111 270.

Top-up TV enables you to see some programmes using a paid-for decoder plus a card at around £8 a month. Channels include UKTV Gold, Food and Style, British Euro Sports, Cartoon Network, Discovery Channel and others. *www.topuptv.com*, 08700 543 210.

Free To Air (also known as FTA, Free-To-Air, In The Clear). Basically all BBC channels are free, but you need a digital receiver. You can buy a new one from any High Street electrical store but I found much cheaper second-hand receivers on eBay.

FreeSat. Sky Digital's name for a one-off £20 card enabling you to view ITV, Channel 4 and Channel 5 through its Sky Digibox. Does away with monthly fees and provides access to over 120 digital TV channels and 80 digital radio channels. *www.freesatfromsky. com,* 0870 240 5651.

Change your bank

Consumers' Association magazine *Which?* claimed in a survey (July 2005) that customers of the big five banks (HSBC, Lloyds TSB, RBS-NatWest, Barclays and Halifax-Bank of Scotland) pay an average of £400 a year on unnecessary charges. These charges are racked up by selling products that customers don't really need, and charging ridiculous sums for small services. Cancelling a cheque costs £50 among the big five, but £30 for Cahoot, an internet bank.

The *Which?* survey put the smaller banks higher in terms of customer satisfaction. Smile topped the list, followed by First Direct, Intelligent Finance, the Co-operative Bank and Nationwide.

Top Tip! You may find that when you call to change your bank, you are offered much better deals to stay, so don't be too hasty. Let them woo you.

Check your savings

There is no point in having savings if they earn you less interest than you pay on credit card debts. Are you getting the best interest rates, and making the most of your tax-free allowance by putting them in an ISA? You can get 'wraparound' ISAs that allow you to put your own mix of investments inside them. Seek independent financial advice by finding a paid-by-the-hour advisor at IFAP, *www.ifap.org.uk*, 0117 971 1177, or IFAS, *www.aifa. net*, 020 7628 1287.

This can be done painlessly by swapping your broker to one who doesn't take commission, or so much commission, allowing more to go into your pension pot.

> **Top Tip!** Hargreaves Lansdowne is a large firm whose Pension Discount Service is on 0117 900 9000, *www.h-l.co.uk*. They claim to offer the best range of initial savings of any UK broker and also offer a Vantage Service which shares renewal commission with you annually – check for details.

Check your car repayment costs

See if you can get a better rate of interest elsewhere. You may well find that you are offered a better rate with a payment holiday of up to four months. *Which*? magazine reported that Barclays charged £1,319 for a £5,000 loan over three years, but its Barclaycard subsidiary only charged £542. See my section on pawnbrokers below, too.

Getting better interest rates

One of the most farcical facts of finance is that rich people get lower interest rates than poorer people, who are seen as a credit risk. I should have thought that making people with less money pay more to borrow it increases the risk that they won't pay it back.

However, you can do certain things to improve the rates you are offered and get higher credit limits. I don't advocate the latter if you are thinking of going on a little spree! (You can turn down automatic credit limit increases, by the way.)

When you apply for credit, the lender will check your credit rating with agencies like Callcredit, Equifax and Experian and give you a score called a Credit Rating. The higher this rating, the lower your interest rate.

You are entitled by law to see a copy of your Credit Rating. It normally costs £2 to apply. If it's wrong, you can ask the holding company to change it. Notorious mistakes in the past include confusing you with others who used to live at your address.

Others you are 'financially connected with' may be taken into account too. Your lender should allow you to choose whether to include 'financial associates' in your application. If you have lived with someone who defaulted in the past, check to see that it is now noted that you are not connected.

The credit check companies don't always hold all information on which credit cards you have. Some credit card companies only log information on people who are in arrears for three months or longer.

The signs that give you a top-score credit rating

You have other active loan or credit card accounts.

I find this hard to understand, but credit grantors prefer 'active' accounts which you are still paying off, to accounts that you have settled. I found this when I moved home and decided to buy an anti-snoring adjustable bed for my husband as a surprise. I had trouble getting credit to buy it in instalments, as I had no loans, so no credit check company had a record of me!

(The bed, which I bought from Dreams, has been a success regarding anti-snoring, but provoked a marital near-disaster as it has two single mattresses which edge apart as the night progresses, causing the sleepers to fall down the hole in the middle.)

You can pay things off over time. Credit grantors prefer to see that you have a credit history – accounts maintained for at least three years.

You have not delayed payments or defaulted. They call this 'having derogatory items in your payment history'.

You have lived in your home for six years. They check the Electoral Roll for this.

You don't have a lot of recent credit searches. If you make over two credit card applications in six months this may well be frowned on as showing that you are overstretched. Other incidental searches, such as for opening a new bank account, don't count.

You have no county court judgments.

You can get a free copy of *Credit Explained*, a government-funded booklet explaining your rights to information held about you, and which affects your credit rating. Call 08456 30 60 60 or go to *www.ico.gov.uk*.

Sell the second car

Or stop using it until you can afford it again. Park it off-road so that you can reclaim part of your road tax and save on insurance. Or get a motorcycle or bicycle.

Pawn something

If you need up to £5,000 for up to six months and have ID and anything from a ring to a computer or car to put down as security, a pawnbroker can be better than a bank loan because the process is fast and there are no early-repayment penalties. If you don't repay your loan after six months, the pawnbroker warns you and then sells your item, giving you the balance if the item fetched more than your loan. You pay interest on your loan at rates higher than credit cards, but they don't charge interest on the interest as credit card companies do. Pawnbrokers are regulated under the Consumer Credit Act so must behave legally. Avoid those who charge a setting-up fee.

The National Pawnbrokers Association can give you a list of local members and sort out grievances. 0118 9477 385, *www.thenpa.com*.

Consolidation loans

These are the ones they advertise on TV, explaining that you lump together all your repayments and get one lower interest rate. Debt counsellors don't like them because they say the interest rates are usually higher than those charged by banks and building societies. Also, they often come with 'built-in payment protection insurance' with terms which may not cover you if you are ill or made redundant. They tend to be secured on your house, which means if you don't repay them, you lose your house.

I don't see why you shouldn't ask for written terms from these loan people, as long as you make a sensible decision eventually. But I have my own objections to the way their ads suggest borrowing yet more money than you owe, to go on holiday, for instance. I beg you not to do that. Particularly telling, to me, is the customer in one ad who referred to his loan application as a 'claim' as if he was applying for insurance or social security to which he was entitled.

Transfer your credit card balance

Rate card tart is considered an unpleasant name but personally I am fond of apple tart so I just think 'yummy' when I hear it. Shop around for the best zero per cent offers and use the money to repay a credit card charging interest.

> **Top Tip!** Never, ever, leave it to the last minute to transfer a zero per cent credit card balance to another zero per cent credit card deal. Credit card companies are getting clever at preventing you from doing this and ... wallop! You cop a huge payment when your zero per cent deal runs out.

Credit card companies are reluctant to tell you the exact date when any zero per cent deal runs out but force it out of them and make a big diary note. Cheat yourself by making that diary note at least four weeks in advance of run-out day. You have to give yourself plenty of time to transfer balances to a new card in case something unforeseen happens.

For instance, if you try to transfer money from your bank to the credit card, they might announce that they have a 'house limit', which means they deliberately limit the sum you can transfer over the phone to them.

The problem with credit card tarting is, the day of reckoning will come sooner or later. You are putting it off. But if you need to put it off, fine, as long as you have a plan in place and are not just dreaming that Father Christmas will descend and pay it off.

"

JANE'S GOLDEN TIP

Comparison services like www.uSwitch.com *provide lists of the best zero per cent deals. If you play the zero per cent game, you must apply for a new card as soon as you see a new deal advertised and at least six weeks ahead of the date you need a new card, to get it in time.*

"

It is possible to make a few hundred pounds on zero per cent balances in order to pay off something else. Check whether the card will put money into your current account. Put it straight into a tax-free ISA savings account. You will make interest on the money. But you have to note the payback date carefully in your diary and repay ten days before that date, or they will charge you interest in full on the whole time.

Before transferring a credit card balance, look out for hidden charges, typically two per cent of the sum capped to £50, just to switch balances. Some companies transfer for free. Phone and ask – don't just transfer and bury your head in the sand, later complaining that you didn't realise.

A zero per cent interest deal gives you time to repay something else. It is NOT a holiday from repaying debts. If you don't make a plan, your debt will increase. See the whole of this book.

Getting your payment priorities right

First, always pay your mortgage, car insurance, road tax and council tax – anything that could result in you losing your home or being taken to court and fined.

Then check which credit card or loan has the highest rate of interest. Pay that first.

Subsidise that payment by asking for a payment holiday from non-essentials like odd little insurance policies you might have, or even your pension. Some pensions have built-in flexibility for you to do this.

Credit cards

Credit cards are magic money. Invisible, almost miraculous access to anything you want, from the Bank of Fairyland. But Fairyland also contains trolls, and they can eat you.

To survive and save money, some people have an 'all or nothing' approach. They put all their credit cards away from temptation and just pay cash.

However, despite their tendency to fuel our 'want it now and darn the consequences' culture, credit cards are also jolly convenient tools and unless you have a shopping-addictive personality, you should have a few.

They are safer than carrying wads of cash around.

They may offer you 'purchase protection' insurance if the thing you buy through them breaks within a few months.

They are useful to book hotel rooms in advance, by quoting the card number as a deposit.

They can offer you discounts on things like holidays if you book through them.

> **Top Tip!** Some cards offer extras like automatic travel insurance. Before going away, get your credit card company to send you a copy of the insurance policy and all the contact details, or it will be pretty useless. Check whether the insurance is activated when you pay for all of your holiday or only some of it, through the card.

Credit cards can also be useful if you have a dispute with a shop about something you have bought with a credit card, or if a supplier goes bust, as the credit card company can be liable to repay your money. Because of this, credit card companies have departments aiming to resolve consumer problems by negotiating with the shop. I have to add, on the two occasions I have asked a credit card to refund money denied to me by a shop, they have suggested that I take the shop to court first.

However, this convenience comes at a hefty price, with most interest rates way higher than the Bank of England base rate. 'At the moment, credit card companies make less than sixty per cent of their profits on interest. The other forty per cent come from penalties levied on people who are either inefficient or in difficulty.' *Malcolm Hurlston, Co-founder, Credit Card Counselling Service*.

Repaying the minimum each month will barely dent your debt. Some cards have reduced the smallest monthly payment to two per cent. At this rate, if you owe the £2,100 average balance at 14.9 per cent APR, it would take you 27 years and five months to clear – not including 'purchase protection' payments which would add months more onto the repayment times.

> **Top Tip!** Think of credit cards as debt cards.

The 'fire and ice' trick

I picture my credit cards as books of matches. They will burn me if I play with fire. If you feel in danger of doing the same, freeze your assets, literally. Get a clean tin, which can't be put in the microwave. Wrap your cards in plastic, add water and place in the freezer. If you want to use them, you will have to defrost them, and that gives you time to reconsider.

Don't let the trolls catch you

However, some credit card companies do offer long-term low interest rates. The cheapest and best deals change constantly, so check a comparison website which tabulates all the deals available, from zero per cent offers to low interest and perks. Try *www. iii.co.uk*, *www.fool.co.uk*, *www.moneysupermarket. com*, *www.creditsearcher.co.uk*, *www.About-Credit-Cards.co.uk*, *www.ukcreditcards247.co.uk* and *www. uSwitch.com*. Most of these sites also carry information about best loan deals. *www.best-prices-uk.co.uk* and *www.thisismoney.co.uk* carry calculators to help you work out how long your loans will take to repay at various interest rates. Check a few. Some carry rather obscure credit cards which may be worth having. If you apply for more than two cards in six months, you're likely to be rejected for a third card, as that is a sign that you may be in deep financial waters, so stop cards which you no longer use before applying.

Check the card's standard interest-free payment time. It may be shorter than you assume. I'm not talking about zero per cent payment deals on cards – we'll get onto them – but the ordinary time between making the purchase and getting the bill. It used to be a standard 56 days, but an increasing number of cards now give you 45 or 46 days. If you don't pay in time, they slam on interest charges backdated to the day you bought the item.

If you have used a zero per cent balance transfer offer to transfer money over from a higher interest card, put the card away and don't use it for purchases unless it includes a zero per cent deal on these too. Cards tend to use your payment to repay the zero per cent balance offer first, racking up interest against your purchases.

Don't incur late-payment charges or you tend to get a £20 'fine'.

> **Top Tip!** Set up a direct debit monthly payment, or write payment dates in your diary.

One nasty little habit that credit card companies can adopt is to be slow at answering the phone if you want to set up a direct debit, hoping presumably that you will give up and then forget. If you do set up a direct debit, they are extremely slow to action it, enabling them to charge you a late-payment fine for the first repayment.

Don't exceed your credit limit – another £20 fine. You can phone the card company and check your balance instantly, so don't bury your head in the sand when out shopping. You can also ask for your credit limit to be increased, even for a few months, though I don't recommend it.

Never write credit card cheques. You are usually charged a two per cent 'handling charge' and interest, even if you repay the money in full on time.

Never withdraw cash on your credit card for the same reason. Don't use any old credit card to get cash abroad. Most 'load' – or 'charge' as I call it – a typical 2.75 per cent on your money. You are probably better off getting cash from your bank account using a debit card in the hole in the wall, as long as your card has a Cirrus or Maestro sign or if your card is labelled Switch, or the Visa sign for Delta. You pay around £1.50 per withdrawal and you get the bank's standard exchange rate – so if you withdraw quite a large sum in one go, you save on commission charges. *Nationwide Gold Card says it does not charge commission on purchases abroad.*

Don't set up regular payments using your credit card rather than your bank account. If you want to cancel the deal, the company you pay has to do it, not you – and if they prove slow to cancel, you pick up the bill.

If your card offers points or 'cashback', use it for all your purchases but pay the bill back in full every month or you will stockpile debt. You receive the cashback payment paid annually, not monthly, so don't rely on it.

Some credit cards offer Air Miles and similar points schemes which mean that if you collect enough, you get free or cheap travel. I have had two family holidays to Italy using Air Miles collected in this way, but usually after several years and after using credit cards for major purchases like computers. Check the comparison websites I have mentioned here for what you can get – it's all listed in tabular form.

Don't use credit cards to impress others. Do you really care if a waiter fawns all over you because he hopes for a big tip? Does the fleeting admiration of a complete stranger in a shop or club really make you feel better about yourself? Even if you do have more money (or rather, credit) than others, it is dangerous to advertise the fact by flashing cards around.

IKEA charges extra to anyone using a credit card in their stores.

Storecards are often the last hope of those who have shot through their credit card limits and are still trying to commit financial suicide by continuing to shop. Nearly half the people who take out credit in shops hadn't planned to do so when they left home.

"

JANE'S GOLDEN TIP

The only use for a storecard is if you have your eye on a big purchase in the sale, like a piece of furniture, and the storecard is offering a percentage off everything you buy on the day you get the card. Take the card, hit them for the sale price minus your discount, then cut the card up and pay the money off quickly.

"

Selling your stuff

So many people seem to have a rusty old car or other vehicle lurking somewhere. You can't sell it because 'the dog likes to sit in it' or you delude yourself that you are about to do it up and make a fortune.

Do yourself a favour. Just sell it. *www.autorola.co.uk*, 01625 507015, will give you a free valuation and list your car. You pay commission of between £100 and £225 only if it is sold.

Also sell that second freezer. (Yes, I have been to your house, down the chimney like a sort of Anti-Santa, looking for things to take away rather than gifts to leave. You were asleep and I didn't wake you.)

You need the money and the space, so it is worth admitting that you will never again wear a floppy hat and a feather boa, nor finish the million-piece jigsaw. You have also moved on from certain hobbies so you might as well sell the trampoline and its matching set of fluffy handcuffs. (We won't ask ...)

When selecting stuff to sell, the cast-iron test is, have you used or worn this for a year? Does it bring you any joy? If you can't or won't make a Sell Pile, get a friend to make a pile of suggested throw-outs. Go through these.

Hurray for eBay!

Charges involve a fee for listing (from 15p) and a percentage of the selling price, plus more for photographs and having your item listed in two different categories. For a guide, check *www.eBay. co.uk* and go to 'help'. To pay the minimum, start simply.

Register first using a credit card. Check what the market is like for the stuff you want to sell, before spending anything to put it up for sale. Most people think their things are worth a good deal more than they really are, unfortunately. But you can have some nice surprises too.

Use 'search' to scan the site for similar items to the one you're selling, then 'advanced search' to eliminate the dross and find the price bracket of your item. It may be that there is no market for it on eBay, in which case see my other suggestions below for turning your junk into cash.

Inside 'search' you will find an icon which emails you so you can track bidding on similar items.

Wrap your item, then weigh it at the post office and get a post-and-packing price. Make your item compact, as postal charges depend on the bulk of the item too now, but also pack it well because if it arrives broken, your buyer may want their money back!

You need up to six photos of your object, loaded onto your computer.

Write a headline, subhead and some description, giving an honest account of any damage. Spell words correctly or buyers won't find you. Avoid pointless puff like 'amazing bargain'. Put in as many keywords as possible that will bring potential buyers in: 'antique blue and white Furnival china cup' will attract collectors of blue and white china, antiques, cups and Furnival china.

Don't fill your ad with hostile warnings like 'no refunds' – you need to be human and nice or it will count against you when the buyer fills out a feedback form rating their transaction with you – which is why it's not a good idea to overcharge for p&p. Gain over five per cent negative feed back and many buyers won't trade with you again.

> **Top Tip!** Look out for eBay's cheap deals for sellers, usually on Thursdays. Time your auction to end on or after Sunday night, when lots of people are bidding.

You can sell an item for a price using 'buy it now' but you stand to make most money from putting something up for a ten-day auction. You need to be around during this time as potential buyers may email questions and you need to answer these, e.g. 'how badly cracked is it?'. If you are polite to a buyer at the beginning, you will build up a loyal customer base.

When the auction closes, an email tells you who your successful bidder is and you receive your money into your credit card through PayPal, eBay's payment system. Yippee – less credit card to pay off this month! The convention is that you send the item within five days unless you warn of some delay.

Escrow is eBay's system used to avoid both buyers and sellers being ripped off when buying or selling at large sums. It holds the buyer's money until the buyer receives the goods and reports that they are happy with them.

Beware a scam in which unsuccessful bidders are emailed offering them the opportunity to buy the item outside the eBay network. They send the money and never receive the goods.

'If you see the price of something you want to sell is not moving, some sellers invent an alternative identity for themselves. They then gently edge the bidding price upwards by putting in a series of small bids until they just cross the other bidder's maximum in the hope that they will butt up their bid one more time. At which time the fictitious buyer withdraws. It isn't quite moral and the danger is, you'll end up selling things to yourself, but it may bring the price up.' *Anonymous seller*.

Car booting

You soon learn the hard way that things that cost loads in a glossy store change hands for a few pounds in the open air. Here's how to do it.

- Start saving all your carrier bags immediately as you will need loads on the day.

- Pinpoint the right sale. Check the local paper. A few weeks before you plan your sale, tour some sites for the ones that attract most customers.

- Ask some sellers if they have covered their pitch fees – around £12 – and if the market is good.

- Check which positions are busiest and ask those sellers what time they arrived to secure their sites. If you can't be bothered, go for a site near a refreshment van but not on top of it, or queues will stop your customers seeing you.

- Compare prices of things you hope to sell.

- Think how to display your stuff. Can you beg or borrow from local churches or Scouts a wallpaper table, clothes rail and lockable cabinet if you have decent jewellery?

- Don't bother to turn up in inclement weather.

"

JANE'S GOLDEN TIP

Save money on tables by laying things out on the ground on a large plastic groundsheet, the kind of thing you can buy to cover furniture when you are painting. If you have one, take a plastic gazebo or even umbrellas against rain. Old clothes-horses are great for displaying curtains, tablecloths and bed linens.

"

The week before the sale

If you don't have much stuff, club together with friends to halve your overheads. You need a fair amount of stuff to sell to make a car boot worthwhile.

Don't leave getting your stuff together until the night before. Wipe, dust or mend anything you plan to sell or people will haggle the price down over a small mark which you could have sponged off at home.

'I wish I had written price tags before I arrived at the sale, and researched prices on the internet, especially for old records, books and china. We had dealers searching for jewellery, old Blue Peter or Rupert Bear annuals, old bibles and Smurf toys!' *Juliet, Norwich.*

> ## JANE'S GOLDEN TIP
>
> *It doesn't matter if your price tags state high prices. People will haggle anyway at a car boot sale and feel they have got a good bargain – yet you know you would have gone lower. Write reduced prices on the tags when the first rush has gone.*

Don't sell Granny's belongings which could have fetched more in an antique and collector's fair at £25 for a table and a calmer atmosphere. Load your car the night before so you are ready for an early start. Park it somewhere safe.

Take lots of wrapping for fragile things and aprons with pockets on the front or a tin with a lid for money, plus 'float' – lots of pound coins, silver and a few fivers. Note how much you started with so you know how much profit you made at the end.

Prepare flasks and food, as you will be tied to your pitch for hours.

On the day

Go to the loo just before setting out. Wear layers of clothing to cope with weather changes. Arrive as early as you can. When the gates open, you may be swamped and, if you are still setting up, some people 'help' by pulling things out of your car and tearing bags apart.

Do not be cowed by these pushy buyers. They are usually dealers, despite their scruffy appearance, and are expert hagglers and they will put your things – and a few more you haven't noticed – into their bags while offering you silly money. A common con is to gather an armful of things and offer a few pounds – concealing hidden riches in the middle before you realise. Or to bargain down a price for one thing, then a second – and offer an even lower price for the two things combined as if doing you a favour!

Around 10am the casual shoppers arrive and will buy your things for a better price.

Keep your 'shop front' looking nice. As you sell things, fill the gaps as people will walk around a few times.

Don't accept £20 notes. Car boot sales are a prime way of disseminating forgeries and they are incredibly difficult to detect. Ask the buyer to change the note elsewhere and come back to you.

> **Top Tip!** Put the naffest and worst-taste things at the front and charge most for them. I got the highest prices on my stand once for a disgustingly ugly wooden gong and a broken china well without a bucket. It's amazing what people will buy.

If you don't want to take anything home, offer your dregs to another stall-holder who does it regularly.

Advertising your things

For one or two items you could try any of the following to advertise your stuff:

- Free postcards on the noticeboards near the tills in supermarkets and big DIY stores like Homebase

- Postcards in sweet-shop windows

- School and church magazines

- Loot, *www.loot.com*, 08700 43 43 43 and *www. exchangeandmart.co.uk*, 0800 680 680

- A specialist club or collectors' magazine, if the items are of specialist interest. Find these by keying in words like 'antique fans' or 'Jaguar' etc. into a search engine like Google. Phone the club magazine editor and ask advice first.

Selling by auction

At the lower end of the auction market are local auctioneers who specialise in the rather sad remains of house clearances – boxes of china, board games, tatty sofas. You are not likely to make much from selling a treasure through them. Do some research. Phone around a few auction houses. Some offer specialist sales and you may be better to wait for those. Register or make an appointment with them in advance, or take your item and queue for a free valuation. (They may visit you for larger pieces of furniture if they are local.) To get the best price, tell the valuer everything you know about your object, no matter how insignificant

– they are like a murder detective, trying to put details into place! Try to get several opinions.

If you sell, the valuer should recommend the minimum 'reserve' price so that you don't give your treasure away for a song. You will also be charged a price to put the item in the sale catalogue plus up to 15 per cent commission on the price your treasure sells for, plus other costs like handling and insurance, and VAT on everything. If the item doesn't sell, you may still have to pay something.

> **Top Tip!** A lot of small, local auctioneers are natural pessimists. Mine always tells me (and my friends, so I know it's not personal!) that any stuff 'won't make more than £15 so it's hardly worth selling'. Then when you see the awful old tat they DO sell, you think, 'Hold on a minute!' I ignored this gloomy auctioneer's advice and received £60 for a hideous vase someone gave me years ago. However, if you feel put-off, tour a few antique shops until you find one that specialises in something you have to sell. Antique shop owners can be awfully fair about prices and if you don't like what you're offered, you need not sell.

The new Fraud Act makes it illegal to gain profit from knowing something and not pointing it out to someone else. That, technically, puts paid to the entire antique trade. But if you sell a painting from your attic that turns out to be a long-lost Titian or something, you might have comeback by pointing out that the buyer who secretly recognised it should have told you what it was and offered you a fair price.

Selling books

Your easiest option may be to take them to a second-hand book dealer for instant cash.

If you have paperbacks to sell, *www.greenmetropolis. com* charges nothing to you to put your books up for sale, at a standard price of £3.75 per book to buyers. If a book of yours sells, you receive £3. Some of the proceeds go to the charity Woodland Trust.

You may get the best price for a book in perfect or near-perfect condition on *www.amazon.co.uk*. Have it ready to send before advertising. My teenager has sold his A-level textbooks in this way and comments that it is much easier than eBay.

Always wrap a book in bubblewrap to post.

> **Top Tip!** If you have a book that's out of print, you may be pleasantly surprised by its worth. It can really rocket, especially for a good hardback, so it's worth covering them in clingfilm or something when you first buy new books to keep them pristine.

> **Top Tip!** When posting books or papers, tell the post office clerk what they are, as there are lower postage rates for printed paper.

DVDs and electronic games

You can sell DVDs, videos sometimes, and games for cash or credits (a more generous deal) to exchange for other movies at Blockbuster, *www.blockbuster. co.uk* for your local store. Also try Choices, *www. choicesvideo.co.uk*, 0870 24 22 800.

Aficionados of this activity tell me that you are likely to get slightly better prices at local independent stores.

Selling your clothes

Will you ever wear your wedding dress again? A bride in China might – apparently, some snap up European wedding clothes. Even a pair of jeans can be sold on eBay (see above).

Children's clothes are particularly good to resell as children grow out of them rather than wear them out. You can do this through the web, often free. Sites like *www.babygurgles.co.uk* specialise in things for the 0-3 age group and, at the time of writing, were offering free sales ads.

www.babywearexchange.com (01506 414026) is a second-hand-and-new web shop for babies', children's and maternity wear. Send them outgrown new or nearly-new clothes, stating your selling price. You get 40 per cent of the sale (50 per cent if you take a credit to buy other things from the site). Send 15 items for a £5 credit. Subscribe to the newsletter to get 10 per cent off your order; and refer five friends to get another £3 off. Save say £15 (£5 credit plus say £10 on baby or children's clothes).

Dress agencies. (See page 157) You take your clean things along to be valued, then once they are sold you receive a percentage of the selling price.

If like me, you bought a few snazzy things BC (before children) – I mean interesting clothes like Quant or Katherine Hamnett – you may be best selling them at auction. Kerry Taylor organises vintage clothes auctions and gives free opinions. 020 8676 4600, *www.kerrytaylorauctions.com*.

www.clothesagency.com, 01285 885283, is a Cotswolds-based clothes barn which sells mainly on the web. Ads cost £1.25 each with no further commission to pay when you sell.

Selling your curtains

Good quality curtains can fetch surprisingly high prices. Don't clean them before offering them for sale: if accepted for sale, the shop will clean them and deduct it from your profit. Try Yellow Pages under 'curtain agencies', or Curtain Exchange, *www. thecurtainexchange.net*.

Branch phone numbers:
Bath – 01225 422078
Newport Pagnell – 01908 218 118
Essex – 01376 561199
Cirencester – 01285 643303

Dulwich – 020 8670 5570
Fulham – 020 7731 8316
Norfolk – 01263 712 724
Somerset – 01823 681281
Bury St Edmunds – 01284 760059
Dublin – (353) 01230 4343.

"

JANE'S TRUE CONFESSION

The curtains left behind by the sellers for us in our new home looked like a shameless hussy's frilly Victorian pantaloons. They weren't interlined – that's an extra stiffening between the curtain and ordinary lining – and they were patterned – making them harder to sell, so I didn't hold out much hope of selling them. But I was awestruck when a curtain agency sold them within three weeks and sent a cheque for £500. The buyer left the frilly tie-backs and extras behind too and didn't want the wooden mounts I offered for free.

"

6

Making extra money

Forget ads in the newspaper saying that you can earn vast sums as a writer or proof-reader. These are selling you courses – and any writer or proof-reader will tell you, it's not that easy or lucrative, or everyone would do it.

The following are suggestions for ways of making money, even if you have no qualifications, skills or time. The ideas here range from jobs that take a few hours to occasional work that you can fit in at weekends, around the school run, or even take a toddler to.

Talking

As a member of a focus group for market research, you spend a few hours discussing anything from beds to baked beans with others. Don't expect more than the occasional job, and a pittance – tales of £100 a session are wildly exaggerated – but you get somewhere to sit out of the cold, saving on home heating, and refreshments, saving on food. You can also earn extra if you use your home for the market research group. Saros (see below) pays you something for suggesting other people suitable for focus groups. The Market Research Society, *www.mrs.org.uk*, lists all market research companies. Also try National Opinion Polls, *www.gfknop.com*, 020 7890 9000; *www.sarosresearch.com,* 0870 240 7923; *www.criteria.co.uk*, 020 7431 4366 and *www.biotrax.co.uk*, 0161 736 7312.

Clicking

www.gozingsurveys.com offers you £25 for completing online surveys. Others to try include American Consumer Opinion, *www.acop.com* and Global Test Market, *www.globaltestmarket.com.* Both will send money in pounds sterling. GTM has developed its own worldwide point scheme called MarketPoints, (once you have 1,000 points they send a local currency cheque) and there is *www.netfreestuff.co.uk* which sends vouchers for filling in its initial questionnaire, for example a free weekend away voucher plus you are entered into prize draws to win bigger prizes each time you complete another survey. Also check out *www.ipoints.co.uk*.

Ticking

If you feel able to hold a checklist and interview people on the street, you can earn around £8 an hour, though budget for woolly vests and gloves when standing in the cold for hours. *www.flow-interactive.com*, 020 7288 0884.

Mystery shopping

Just promise me you won't buy anything while you are acting as a spy, reporting on the tidiness, staff behaviour, or what-have-you at clubs, shops, restaurants or pubs. You can earn anything from £7 per visit to £100 a day. Try it.

www.fieldfacts.com, 020 7908 6600;

www.ukims.co.uk, 0870 701 0866;

www.mysteryshopagency.com, 020 8325 8974; and *www.retaileyes.co.uk*, 01908 328 000.

Competing

If you have the time, try your luck at *www.loquax. co.uk*. Registration is free at this portal that lists all the major competitions and updates the list daily. As does *www.Win4Now.co.uk* and *www.instantwin4now. co.uk*.

Gardening

The slickly-named 'Women Returners to Amenity Gardening Scheme' places learners in private gardens for 15 hours a week, paying £58.80. For information, call the Women's Farm and Garden Association, 01285 658339.

Exploiting your car

www.ad-wraps.co.uk (020 7534 5490) provides you with a free car if you are deemed the right kind of ambassador for certain brands. Or they may pay between £66 and £200 per month to wrap your car in an all-over ad, which they point out protects against body damage. Ask if you're suitable.

Renting a room

You can do this, even to your teenager, and need not pay tax on the first £4,250 of rent.

www.mondaytofriday.com is a website for people seeking, and advertising, weekday tenants who go back to their real homes every weekend.

When a lodger moves in, you must tell your insurers, although you won't be covered if their things are stolen or they are light-fingered.

www.LandlordLaw.co.uk can help you draw up a simple agreement with a tenant or lodger.

Renting your home as a film or TV location

It can be unique or quite ordinary-looking – one lady rents out her late husband's garage, as he left it immaculately stacked with bottles and tins and it has atmosphere. You need to live in a quietish area without planes overhead, parking for lorries the size of large removal vans, and good transport links.

You can earn between £250 and £2,000 in a day, depending on whether someone wants a room for a day or a full-scale commercial in your back garden.

It can be fun. However, the downside is that it is the most massive upheaval. You cannot get on with anything while you have up to 25 people hanging around (make-up artists, wardrobe, scene shifters, Uncle Tom Cobley and all).

Although they are strictly contracted not to leave a scrap of paper behind, some do more. I let a new film company into my home for the weekend and ended up with scratched wooden flooring where they had used heavy cameras on rails without putting down protective boarding first, and scuffs on the walls where they had stuck paper on to change the wall colour. All this had to be put right and charged for, with concomitant hassle and expense.

Also, keep your neighbours sweet. If you have a shared drive, I seriously suggest giving them some money as a goodwill gesture. Otherwise, if they see you making dosh, and imagine that you are having fun hobnobbing with famous film stars, they can complain to the local council and get you into trouble.

Don't pay anyone money to put your house up as a location. Proper location agencies don't charge upfront, but take a commission, and most councils have a 'film officer' to keep a list of properties.

See *www.locations-uk.co.uk* and *www.oic.co.uk*, 020 7419 1949.

Also *www.ukfilmcouncil.org.uk*, 020 7861 7861 and your appropriate regional screen agency: Derbyshire, Leicestershire, Lincolnshire, Northamptonshire, Nottinghamshire, Rutland: EM-Media, 0115 934

9090, *www.em-media.org.uk*; Greater London: Film London, 020 7387 8787, *www.filmlondon. org.uk*; Cumbria, Durham, Teeside, Tyne & Wear, Northumberland: Northern Film and Media, 0191 269 9212, *www.northernmedia.org*; Cheshire, Greater Manchester, Lancashire, Merseyside: North West Vision, 0151 708 2967, *www.northwestvision.co.uk*; Bedfordshire, Essex, Cambridgeshire, Hertfordshire, Norfolk, Suffolk: Screen East, 01923 495051, *www. screeneast.co.uk*; Berkshire, Buckinghamshire, City of Oxford, Hampshire, Isle of Wight, Kent, Surrey, Sussex, Channel Islands: Screen South, 01753 656412 *www.screensouth.org*; Birmingham, The Black Country, Herefordshire, Shropshire, Staffordshire, Warwickshire and Worcestershire: Screen West Midlands, 0121 766 1470, *www.screenwm.co.uk*; Yorkshire, Humberside: Screen Yorkshire, 011 3294 4410, *www.screenyorkshire.co.uk*; Cornwall, Devon, Dorset, Gloucestershire, Somerset, Wiltshire: South West Screen, 0117 952 9977, *www.swscreen.co.uk*; Northern Ireland Film & Television Commission, 028 90 233 444, *www.niftc.co.uk*. Scottish Screen, 014 1302 1700/1723/1724, *www.scottishscreen. com*; Wales Screen Commission, 0800 849 8848, *www.walesscreencommission.co.uk*.

Renting out your land or outbuildings

If you can keep your grass growing and have at least an acre of spare land, with fencing and shelter, you can rent it out as grazing for a horse for at least £10 a week. The British Horse Society will help,

08701 20 22 44, *www.bhs.org.uk*. You can rent out your spare barn, workshop or garage if it has natural light. *www.property.org.uk* carries ads from artists and craftspeople seeking places to work, to rent. You should search the 'properties wanted' section.

Lying down naked for art's sake

Few of us possess the face and body of fashion models – though if you want to get into that, haunt Top Shop at London's Oxford Circus every Saturday where scouts are looking, or the BBC Clothes Show at the International Exhibition Centre in Birmingham, where the big model agencies all have pitched sites which you can approach. However, people of all ages and shapes are in demand as artists' models at your local College of Art or College of Further Education. You just have to be able to sit or lie still and you get up to £11 per hour nude and £8 clothed.

Acting naturally

If you can travel to a studio early in the morning, you can earn from £64.50 to £200 a day as a film extra. You don't need film-star looks – in fact, the more ordinary you are the better, as you will be asked to stand at a bus stop or walk the dog – but you must not giggle or shout 'Hello Mum' when the camera rolls. Expect lots of waiting. Try *www.castingcollective.co.uk*, 020 8962 0099 or *www.rayknightcasting.co.uk*, 020 7722 4111.

Giving of yourself

To donate sperm, you must be under forty and fit. Payments for sperm are rapidly dying out as they are deemed unethical and a recent report recommended paying reasonable expenses and loss of earnings only, defeating your object. Some places may still pay, however, up to £25 a time; check your nearest university's medicine faculty notice board or find a fertility clinic or sperm bank through The Human Fertilisation and Embryology Authority, 020 7291 8200, *www.hfea.gov.uk*, or *www.mannotincluded.com*.

Giving blood

Laboratories will pay about £60 for 600ml of your blood and £5 for your travel costs. This is not the same as donating your blood free at a local donation clinic or mobile van for which you get a free biscuit and a cup of tea. To find your closest session call 0845 7711 711 or enter your postcode at *www.blood.co.uk*. Alternatively see BBC2 Ceefax page 465.

Being a guinea pig for science

You need not be in perfect health, and can be any age, depending what the test requires, to test anything from drugs to face cream to contact lenses for between £80 and £200. The downside is, there might be unpleasant side-effects.

You must judge whether to go ahead for yourself. There are also psychological tests – things like memory games – for which it is worth asking at your nearest university psychology faculty. Try *www.biotrax.co.uk*, 0161 736 7312, for details of trials all over the UK. For £20 you can buy their fuller directory of medical testing centres and surveys going on. Also try *www.gpgp.net, www.hotrecruit. com* (search 'crazy jobs' for relevant info) and the Common Cold Centre, Cardiff, *www.cardiff.ac.uk/ biosi/associates/cold/hctrial/html*, 02920 874099 (or search their website for Common Cold trials). Clinical Neuroscience Research, Dartford, Kent, 01322 286862 *www.psychmed.org.uk*. Manchester's School of Psychiatry and Behavioural Sciences, *www. medicine.man.ac.uk* (keywords = research+volunteer), 0161 306 6000. Each survey has its own contact numbers. Also check your local university's medical faculties.

Watching out for trouble

Become a football club steward and help out a club by watching the crowd during match days. This pays between £20 and £40 for four hours. Contact your local club's safety officer.

Sitting on an advisory board

This is the *crème de la crème* of occasional jobs. There are 30,000 part-time paid jobs on government advisory boards which fall vacant regularly. For a relatively handsome sum, if you have experience of a certain trade or they like the cut of your jib, you could spend a few days a year sitting on committees running hospitals, trade boards or even wine-testing for the Government Hospitality Advisory Committee! Try the office for the Commissioner for Public Appointments, *www.ocpa.gov.uk* or telephone 020 7276 2626, or email *public.appointments.unit@cabinet-office.gov. uk*.

Giving parties

When selling stuff to friends and neighbours, trust your intuition. You may have to make a substantial outlay to buy the stock, and the glossy predictions of huge sales may not come true. However, here are some of the main companies.

Virgin Vie – cosmetics and jewellery, *www. virgincosmetics.com*, 0845 300 8022. Pay £25 and £140 for registration fees, either one-off payments or in instalments.

Formative Fun – educational toys, *www.formativefun. com*. 0845 890 0609. You earn 25 per cent of value of any sales you make at parties or direct; ten per cent if your customer places their order online or by mail order. £25 outlay for 60 catalogues and stationery plus a day's training.

Kleeneze – cleaning products, health and beauty, *www.kleeneze-team.co.uk*, 08703 336688. Twenty-one per cent commission plus possible bonuses on all orders you receive through door-dropping catalogues. Start-up costs from £75 for registration and catalogues.

Avon – cosmetics, bathing, jewellery, and a few clothes, *www.avonuk.com*. Rather secretive, so I pretended to want to join and received an email telling me that there is a joining subscription of £15 deducted from your first two orders, then you have to sell a minimum of £68 of goods, to receive 24 per cent commission, with 30 per cent commission for orders over £128.

> ## JANE'S GOLDEN TIP
>
> *I have been an Avon lady in an attempt to make ends meet and made a loss. This seems most profitable if you live on a large housing estate full of bored and moneyed women or if you work in a large office.*

The Gift Experience – soft toys, novelties, photo albums, candles, jewellery etc., *www.tnjp.co.uk.,* 01691 624672. Send £90 for the initial £180-worth stock, which can be deducted from your commission as you go along. Earn 20 per cent on all sales plus monthly bonus.

Tax on extra income

Naturally you should pay tax on your earnings, even if they are cash.

Money you can claim off your tax bill, in connection with your extra earnings, includes:

- Travel – bus, train, planes, bicycle, whatever, and part of your car running costs and petrol, also parking charges.

- Part of your phone bill. Some of your council tax, insurance and utility bills.

- Research materials (books, papers, magazines you might buy).

- Equipment, like stationery, computers and ink cartridges and any special protective clothing.

Treat collecting receipts as a savings game. When you fill out a tax return, these are taken away from your earnings and you are taxed on the remainder, so the more receipts you collect, the better. See my section on tax for more details, page 43.

For a comprehensive and inspirational guide to all sorts of other work, from casual to starting a business, see *A Bit on the Side: 500 ways to boost your income* by Jasmine Birtles, published by Piatkus, £10.99, or free from the library.

For an awful warning about which jobs not to take, including a very funny account of what it's like to be a sex-line call answerer, see *The Idler Book of Crap Jobs*, edited by Dan Kieran, published by Transworld, £9.99, or free from the library.

Top Tip! Keep a record of what you are paid and – this is totally vital – your expenses, keeping all your receipts in a shoe-box and a running total in a book to save time. Keep these receipts for up to seven years (depending on what type of business you are running), as this is how long the Inland Revenue can demand to look back, if you are unfortunate enough to be 'investigated' for potential tax back-payments. Visit *www.hmrc.gov.uk*, call the tax hotline on 0800 77 88 87 or pick up or download leaflet SABK4, a guide to record keeping.

7

The secrets of shopping and saving

First, get the right mindset. Sorry to spoil your fun, or the feeling that you are naughty but nevertheless thoroughly deserve everything that you want, but when we venture to the shops we are not princes and princesses with infinite time and money. We are busy and important people, with more pressing things to do than to shop all day. Shopping is not our *raison d'être* but merely a way of getting hold of life's necessities.

The last time I went shopping in a department store was two years ago. I can't say I feel culturally or socially deprived. I suffer less from 'analysis paralysis', the panic we feel when faced with too many choices in a shop. What's analysis paralysis? For instance, toothpaste. Large, small, pump, sensitive, bicarbonate of soda, anti-cavity, minty, stripey, for teeth over 40. Then there are three for the price of two and two for the price of one. Or Boots Basic at 27p. If you can't decide, give up and go home.

How to cut your shopping costs - the skills that can save you thousands

The Golden Tips

Never use shopping as a habitual pastime or entertainment unless you are extremely strong-willed and leave your credit cards behind. (You aren't and you won't – who are you kidding?!)

Dump the idea that it is OK to go shopping in discount or factory shops. *People think they are frightfully clever to go there, but I think only an idiot pays full price for most things these days. Discount places are not the natural home of any disciplined money-saver.*

If you go shopping, you don't have to buy anything. *'Just looking' is your mantra. If you go out shopping and return empty-handed, congratulations. It means that you are a discriminating shopper, not a pushover, not a punter, and not easy meat for marketing experts to manipulate.*

'I went to buy a handbag/drill bit/pair of medium-size rubber gloves but there was nothing to suit me in the shops,' is the war cry of smart shoppers.

Returning empty-handed actually shows that you are fully in control of your money as a shopper rather than frittering … and you know how we hate fritterers!

You can waste money on cheap things as easily as on designer chic. *Never get into the habit of thinking, 'I'll buy this, even if I don't like it/need it. It's only a few pounds.' If you get on a bus and you* can't pay the fare – even if you are one penny short – you don't ride. Do supermarkets let you have things if you don't give them all the money? So that money you wasted would have been handy. Think how much more handy it would be to pay off those credit cards.

Finally, don't let other people put you off. Your abstemiousness may make them feel uncomfortable about that little pair of earrings they bought at lunchtime, so they act the agent provocateur, like the person who offers you chocolates when you're dieting. If anyone around you at home or work dares to make any critical comment about you coming back empty-handed but full-pursed, it is none of their darn business. Tell them I say they are sillies.

"
JANE'S MOST GLEAMING GOLDEN TIP
Don't go shopping unless you really have to.
"

FIRST AND FOREMOST, GET IT FOR FREE. *www. freecycle.org/groups/unitedkingdom* is a message board on which anyone can offer anything they have, free. Buyer collects. Start by going to the main web page, which is American, then work backwards to the page for your home town, e.g. freecycle-brighton, hullfreecycle (visitors need to register before typing in required location).

To stop yourself being overwhelmed with messages, fill in the profile indicating what you are interested in and press 'digest' to get your emails in a batch.

For random free gifts, try *www.freebies.com*, *www. freebieholics.co.uk*, and *www.freeukstuff.net*. For many of these freebies you have to fill out a questionnaire. If your friends are happy for you to pass on their details, you can also get freebies from *www.referralfreebies.co.uk*.

Also check *www.britishfreebies.co.uk*, *www. bigmoneyleague.co.uk,* *www.greasypalm.co.uk,* *www.luckysurf.co.uk*. I particularly like *www. top50freebies.co.uk* which offers cash back from fifty companies and extra freebies like a cinema ticket voucher when you sign up.

Think around the problem before throwing money at it

For instance, buying drinks when you are out can cost a fortune. Cold drinks can cost around £2. Take a flask or refill a cool-looking bottle at home with tap water. Asking for tap water in a café or pub is free and I find waitresses understand. A surprising number of shops offer free drinks in hot weather. Large furniture stores, estate agents and car showrooms are all good. The latter are also good for hot coffee, soup and tea. Starbucks offers free muffin tasters.

Alternatives to buying

Join stores' loyalty clubs for discounts. Boots Advantage Card is the best value. If you join special interest groups, like Boots Parenting Club (08450

708090), you will get extra points on big purchases like nappies.

Can you buy it second-hand or at a cheap auction? Check jumble sales, charity shops, eBay, *www.loot.com*, *www.exchangeandmart.co.uk*, small auctioneers, car boot sales, garage sales, local papers; or put an ad in your local freesheet newspaper or in a sweet-shop window for about 60p: remarkably effective and under-used.

The Salvation Army tends to hold weekly jumble sales at local centres where you get the best bargains of the three for £1 variety. Check in Yellow Pages or Thomson's Local for your nearest.

> **Top Tip!** When searching for phone numbers, the Phone Directory books are still free. So is *www.192.com*. Any 0870 number costs you extra money to dial. The website *www.saynoto0870.com* may supply the alternative normal phone number. Or if it's a company, evade the more costly corporate phone numbers that begin 08, by putting its name into a search engine like Google and finding the head office, then phoning in and asking to transfer to the service team.

Auction News is a monthly magazine detailing auctions carried out by official receivers and the police at which you may net anything from a house to a washing machine, for a song. *www.auctionnews. co.uk*, 01332 551300.

Government Auction News is a monthly newsletter devoted to over 100 UK auctions per month including Ministry of Defence vehicles and Customs seizures. *www.ganews.co.uk*.

Greasby's of Tooting, 020 8672 2972, sells at around a third of their value things like pushchairs, musical instruments and camcorders which have been left unclaimed in London Transport's lost property section. *www.greasbys.com*.

www.auctionguides.co.uk lists lots of auctions.

> **Top Tip!** You don't have to attend an auction to bid. You can leave a written bid – but phone and get the item immediately or you rack up storage charges. Ask what the auctioneer's rates are. They add a 'buyer's premium' or small percentage to the winning bid which you have to pay on top of the price, so take account of that when deciding how much to bid.

Use your initiative and ask people. I wanted four tables and cheap shops like IKEA didn't have anything suitable. I saw some in a catalogue, but at nearly £1,000. Eventually I decided to buy cheaper trestle tables. Trestles, new, cost £120. By calling around local catering firms and asking if they had any tables to sell, I bought them at £40 each.

Can you get someone else to buy it for you? Do you have a birthday coming up, or can you feign illness so effectively that someone will buy you something nice to your specification? Or can you convince a friend that THEY need this item in their life and get them to buy it and lend it to you?

Can you get your employer to buy it for you on business expenses? You may be able to make a case for books, magazines or stationery or computer equipment. See my section on tax perks in 'lumps and bumps of life'. You may be able to get computers, mobile phones for all the family, bicycles, food and more tax-free.

Can you get it through the state? (I said the state, not the States! Don't venture to America to buy things. The travel costs a fortune and you may have to pay customs duty.) What I mean by the state is:

- If it's a book, DVD or CD, you can order it from your local library. If they can't get it for you, you pay a few pence and they will buy it for you. The advantages of this include not having to pay for expensive shelving at home to store it permanently.

- Many local authorities run toy libraries. Like a book library, but for toys. Aimed at childminders, they are often open to everyone who asks.

- Join a local College of Further Education, even for an evening class, and you will be able to use, free, their internet and broadband facilities and library, and read their newspapers and magazines.

- You can even get free bin bags and garden rubbish collections via your library now. I pay £1 per garden rubbish bag, fill it with what I can't compost, and every two weeks it's collected free, and the bag returned.

- Some areas offer free water butts or composters. Ask your local water board or local authority.

I don't do second-hand, it's dirty

People use this excuse to buy something more expensive and clean in a new carrier bag. Don't make me laugh. Stuff in antique shops, sales etc. is often lovingly cleaned. If not, all you have to do is polish it.

On the other hand, many well-known and expensive shops lend their stock, including bras and knickers, to fashion models and favoured clients for the evening. I have seen girls receiving bags of stuff, trying things on and concealing the price-tags down their backs as they wear the dresses for the evening, then discarding them on the floor afterwards. The next day, those dresses and underwear are replaced on the shop's rails for customers to buy.

Have you checked your local dump? Things there are not always dirty. Before taking things away, you may have to give the staff a small sum. I gave £3 for a William Morris fabric-covered Chesterfield chair recently.

Gardeners, you can sometimes get free compost at dumps, if you take a bag and cart it away yourself.

Have you looked in skips? Skip-hunting is not what it used to be, but you never know, especially in classier areas. Up-and-coming areas are also good, as are business streets just after office hours. It is against the law to take anything without the owner's consent, of course.

Can you buy a cheaper alternative?

You don't need a luxury carpet when you can paint the floor with floor paint and put down a mat. You just need conviction and style. I once knew a couple who kept their food in an old filing cabinet. The 'B' drawer was for bread, 'C' was for cakes and so on.

> **Top Tip!** Some colours are cheaper than others. Why are grey trousers cheaper than black? You would think that as they make black trousers by the millions that THEY would be the cheapest. Read through all the options before buying anything.

Can you make it?

Things don't have to look shop-perfect. We needed garden tables for a party. (Why is it that we always seem to need tables? But we do…) Have you seen the prices of these things these days? We happened to have a large wooden crate used to deliver bricks.

We turned it upside down. Covered it with a pretty cotton tablecloth, £2 from the local charity shop. Instant garden table.

Swap baby wipes for tap water and cotton wool. Exchange fabric softener for a tablespoon of vinegar in the washing machine's final rinse.

Make fruit drinks. Float apple slices in a water jug in the fridge. Tesco Apple Flavoured Spring Water, 69p for 1.5 litres. 1 Tesco Value apple, 12p.

Buy only by Internet

This has many money-saving advantages. You tend to get discounts. You evade parking charges, petrol, incidental purchases like ice creams and coffee and save time on going shopping. Check shops' websites for bargain deals that aren't in the shops. *www.allshopsuk.co.uk/shops/offers* has a handy directory of online deals.

> **Top Tip!** Always check the shop site's bargain section or look for the location of their 'end of the line' shop and call them to see what they have.

> **Top Tip!** Don't automatically believe 'we match cheapest prices' promises. There is usually a get-out in the small print, such as 'except on Wednesdays' or 'except when a competitor's price is cheaper' or something …

Price comparison websites

Check these out on your library's computer, free. These sites show what they claim is the best price for anything you're planning to buy. You can make interesting discoveries. For instance, a local small appliance shop may be cheaper than Tesco or Argos for a washing machine by the time you take delivery charges into account.

It is really worth checking out a few comparison websites as not all of them carry the same information and some also carry second-hand offers.

www.comparestoreprices.co.uk
www.pricerunner.co.uk
www.planetonline.com
www.dealtime.co.uk
www.pricemonkey.co.uk
www.abcaz.com
www.mysimon.com
www.kelkoo.co.uk
www.compareandreview.co.uk.
www.thesimplesaver.com
www.abargain.co.uk

If you intend buying something expensive, you might sign up to *www.greasypalm.co.uk*, a discount website offering cash-back – usually up to five per cent – every time you shop online through it, at all sorts of well-known High Street and discount eShops. Other benefits include money-off coupons and £7 for referring others. I understand that the minimum sum you must earn is £25 before they send it. There is nothing to say that the companies signed up to this are the cheapest, so do your sums rather than be seduced by the thought of money-back.

> **Top Tip!** Can you download a discount voucher or find a discount code to use before you buy? Try *www.wishvalue.co.uk*, *www.instantcouponz.com*, *www.couponmountain.co.uk*, *www.offers.co.uk* and *www.freebies.co.uk*.

www.couponsrule.com gives you money-off vouchers and other money-saving tips, like the current best buys to earn the maximum loyalty points from stores like Boots.

Beware of buying things from abroad. You may have to pay additional shipping costs and custom charges, and if you want to return something, it becomes costly and time-consuming, with your legal rights being harder to establish and pursue.

> **Top Tip!** You should return anything within seven days of receiving it to be sure of getting a refund. I always send things by registered post in case the company claims they got lost.

www.letsbuyit.com allows buyers to group together to get a bulk discount on electronics. It works on economies of scale; so everyone enjoys a lower price created by bulk-buying.

I don't recommend using TV auction or lowest-bid channels. If you're feeling tired or weak especially, I think it's too easy to get carried away by the feeling that everyone else is buying an item and so must you. Then you can become a shopping addict.

"

JANE'S GOLDEN TIP

Check delivery charges before agreeing to buy. Try to get delivery free, saving typically £30. Companies may appear to offer good deals but the delivery charge makes them more expensive.

"

Don't assume eBay is the cheapest website. People become very boring about eBay, as if it were an all-purpose solution to every need. If you have weaned yourself off going to the shopping centre, please don't become an eBay addict instead. New things can be just as expensive there as elsewhere. eBay is good if you need something obscure, like a wheelchair, or spare parts for obsolete cars or motorbikes. Regular internet traders may offer better deals, so shop around using price comparison sites like the ones listed above.

"

JANE'S GOLDEN TIP

eBay is a collector's paradise, but if you're trying to save money, you shouldn't be a collector.

"

Getting the best from buying on eBay

Get up early on Mondays. Few people bid in auctions ending then. Avoid popular times like Sunday nights.

Bid at the last minute. Otherwise you force the price up as you bid against others.

Try to buy from UK-based sellers. It keeps your p&p prices low, and it is harder to get satisfaction from traders overseas.

Shop out of season. Buy ski-wear in July when few people want it.

Avoid the words 'as in' in the small print. These mean the item has flaws and you have no right of return.

Don't confuse buying a product with bidding for information about how to buy a product, sometimes called 'secret sites'. These are famous scams.

Enter every spelling variation you can imagine, including abbreviations and removing spaces between words. Others won't bother.

Get to know the site. The shops page *www.stores.ebay.co.uk* has a directory of specialist microsites which are shop windows with their own unique web addresses within eBay.

Spend some time visiting the various eBay chat-rooms and find out what established users are saying about other buyers and sellers. You can learn a lot and it may even put you off buying an item altogether.

Cheap tricks to save you money whilst shopping

Take your own carrier bags with you and insist the shops put things in them. This is reverse psychology in action. That expensive face-cream just does not seem worth buying when carried in a much-used supermarket plastic carrier, does it?!

Don't buy basics that are packaged in gimmicky ways. You pay more for the drink with the funny nozzle or the pump toothpaste, so stick to a bottle and a tube.

When buying major things, don't pay upfront if you don't need to. Put down a deposit if you have to. If you have second thoughts, it's easier to backtrack than to reclaim cash – and it encourages the shopkeeper to come up with the order too.

Be suspicious of bargains that are too good to be true. They are and there is a reason.

Getting discounts

Elton John may be famous for his high-spending habits, but Geri Halliwell, the former Spice girl, once confessed to a newspaper that she loves asking for discounts as her father was a car dealer, adding that the worst that can happen is that the shop says no. A splendid attitude. Lots of well-off people do this, even in the smartest shops. One professional 'personal shopper' who conducts rich people around shops told me that she is embarrassed and hides behind coat racks while her millionaire client negotiates discounts.

Be friendly when asking for a discount. Look a salesperson in the eye and strike up a relationship.

Ask for money off in return for paying cash. Find the manager, not the Saturday assistant, or any assistant with a bitter and mean mouth (you'll recognise what I mean). Speak quietly as they won't want other customers to hear. You need not carry the cash around with you there and then, but showing a few notes tends to have a magical relaxing effect on shop managers.

> **"**
>
> ### JANE'S GOLDEN TIP
>
> *Don't feel second-best or that the shop is doing you a favour. On the contrary, you should be treated like royalty. The shop makes a sale, so meets its sales targets – usually unrealistic sums dreamed up by head office honchos. And it saves the savage cost of processing credit cards or cheques, without waiting for the money to clear into their account.*
>
> **"**

Suggest a reason for the discount. Are you buying lots of things? An unpopular colour, which would be left on the shelf? Can you take your purchase away there and then? My husband has been known to use a wheelbarrow to take things away from shops. Offer to buy a damaged or torn item, for a larger discount. You have to build up the inconvenience to you and the impossibility that it will ever be quite perfect. Are you a regular shopper? Thanks to my local Budgens, where someone once asked me, 'Would you mind accepting a 15 per cent discount because you shop here a lot?' Would I mind?!

Shop near closing time or during inclement weather. If it is very hot, or there is a storm, they will have had a bad trading day and are more amenable to negotiating.

Don't look well-off. A great antique-dealer's trick, this. A friend of mine had a job designing holiday apartments for Arab princes. Most of her time, she had to source identical bedrooms in different colours for their various wives, but she once decided to refurbish a bathroom in the plushest style. She was in a shop looking at solid-gold bath taps and had forgotten her rather shabby attire, when the assistant conducted her away, saying, 'Madam could never afford those prices; here are the cheaper ones.' He made the mistake of judging by appearances. The irony is that she was trying to spend as lavishly as possible rather than save.

Make a proposal. 'I don't want to pay that for a sofa,' said one smart shopper at a large warehouse-style furniture shop. 'I want to pay this.' They accepted his offer. But he was a literary agent, used to brokering multi-thousand pound deals, so perhaps he exuded an air of authority.

Shop with an OAP. They sometimes get a sympathy vote but can be wily or winning when it comes to asking for money off. Incentivise them by offering to split the discount you get as a result of their fronting the deal. Among shops which give over-60s a discount are Wyevale Garden Centres, 0800 413 213, *www.wyevale.co.uk* and Focus DIY centres, 01270 501555, *www.focusdiy.co.uk*.

Effective complaining

It's always worthwhile to make a complaint, as long as you don't make it fruitlessly.

Know your cut-off limits. Have in your head an idea of how much your time is worth.

Don't waste money-making hours and your phone bill hanging on, particularly if you are self-employed.

Alternatively, keep a notebook and pencil by the phone to record all the times and dates you called; whom you spoke to and what they said. This kind of detail is invaluable when complaining, especially if you have to take the company to court.

Know what you want before you begin: a refund, credit note, extra money? If you are fed up with call centres, obtain the headquarters phone number of the company and ask to speak to the Managing Director's personal assistant. They normally get things done.

If you have reached an impasse, consult your local Trading Standards Officer, available through your local authority, free. You can get their contact details via *www.tradingstandards.gov.uk* too, and also try *www. consumerdirect.gov.uk*.

Goods bought from a shop must be fit for the purpose for which they were bought, match any description that is given and be of satisfactory quality.

When complaining, I have found it worth quoting The Sale of Goods Act 1979/1994, Trades Description Act 1968 and Consumer Credit Act 1974, a recital which seems to unnerve shop staff. I can't imagine why. For more details on these, visit *www.dti.gov.uk* or ask the Citizens Advice Bureau.

Trade Associations usually act, in the last resort, for their members who pay them rather than you. Even if they say they have complaints procedures, don't expect much and you will be pleased if you get more.

If you want to complain about services like the phones – and who doesn't? – look up the ombudsman for your particular service at your library, in the phone book or on the web. They are slow but free. Don't involve a lawyer before dealing with them or you will have spent money and the ombudsman may say they can't deal with your case.

> **Top Tip!** You get the best service from an ombudsman if you can send copies of letters or emails, ask for reasonable remedies rather than huge 'compensation' and don't dress your letter up pompous language – words like 'notwithstanding' – but tell the story simply. My husband recently complained to the Financial Ombudsman about Morgans Independent Advisers, who did not draw out some pension money he wanted on time, and did not send him the right forms when he complained. It took the ombudsman eight months or so to deal with this, but the service was free, unstressed and effective. Morgans were told to pay interest to my husband at a high rate on his delayed money and an extra £300 as a gesture of their regret.

www.bbc.co.uk has useful information including, in the Watchdog section, how to complain and letters to download and personalise.

www.howtocomplain.com is a free, independent site which claims that over 76 per cent of complaints made through it have been resolved, mainly in the consumer's favour.

www.financevictims.co.uk offers help on complaining about financial institutions. Also try the Financial Services Authority, *www.fsa.gov.uk*, 0845 606 1234.

Before buying legal advice, check your home insurance policy and your union, which often have advice lines free.

For consumer advice, I recommend the *Which?* Legal Service, *www.which.net*, 0845 307 4000 or 01992 822800, £12.75 for three months' membership, with £3 off for *Which?* Magazine subscribers, or check for special offers. Citizens Advice Bureaux, *www.adviceguide.org.uk*, have leaflets on consumer rights and may offer specific help. The Office of Fair Trading, *www.oft.gov.uk*, 08457 22 44 99, also offers leaflets on consumer rights. I have found them unwilling to offer specific advice and get the impression that they tend to concentrate on the larger legal issues of trading in Britain.

www.haveyoursay.com is a shining example of direct action. Its founder had problems with his Land Rover and was unimpressed with the way they were handled. He began a 'blog', a kind of web diary, of complaints which turned into a consumer discussion site so influential that Land Rover ended up asking him to take a new car, as long as he would remove the site. The site remains and is worth looking at for those who would follow suit.

Smart savings on food

To save money this month, I want you to use up the food you already have at home, rather than shopping for more food. *All of it.*

"

JANE'S GOLDEN TIP

You can tell an expensive food shop without going in. Check for a stripped wooden floor.

"

Is this you?

I have found that the worst overspenders tended to have two freezers full of food, even if they were a household of two. They still went shopping every week in supermarkets, which they treated as a social jaunt. They also had extras like meat delivered.

Another characteristic that overspenders share is a high use of takeaways and ready-prepared food. Often, they have given up the effort (or pleasure) of cooking proper food, or as one girl put her addiction to microwave meals, 'I only cook it if it pings.' Once they rediscovered the joys of food, they saved loads.

An easy way to save?

Stop eating out for the month and *take away the takeaways*. You can feed a family for a week for the cost of one moderately-priced restaurant bill.

Try not to overstock with food as if your life depended on it.

If you have a freezer the size of a stretch limo, sell it. It takes money to run, you tie up cash stocking it up – and unless you live deep in the country, it is healthier to buy fresh food more often. For the past three years, I have fed a family of five using a tabletop freezer inherited from my mother. It has not affected the quality of our life one jot.

If children complain that their favourite things aren't always available under your new smart spending regime, point out that you are not a short-order chef running a restaurant for them.

> **Top Tip!** Look out for any supermarket range which is plainly packaged and labelled 'basic' or 'budget', such as Sainsbury's excellent Basic range.

Buy the food you really eat, and eat what you buy

Research reveals that all UK households throw away a third of all the food we buy. (Source: Waste and Resources Action Programme.)

Sixty-one per cent of households confessed to throwing away a soggy lettuce each week because they thought they would eat more salad than they do. (Source: Prudential survey.)

If you throw stuff away, take the hint and don't buy any more of the same.

Have a freezer audit. Go down to the bottom and use what is lurking there. Take the opportunity to defrost your freezer. It will save electricity if it doesn't have more icicles growing in it than Santa's grotto at Harrods.

Make food shopping into a game. Challenge yourself, or whoever is food shopping for you, to buy an entire week's groceries only buying special offers or marked-down things. It is strangely satisfying to succeed. Or make shopping into an inter-family contest each week: who can buy the same basics and come home with the lowest bill? Display each person's bill on the family notice board or fridge.

Don't be a supermarket snob. It's a bit Hyacinth Bouquet to care where you buy your things, and in my price comparisons, the most prestigious stores averaged 50p extra per pack on basic things like cat food, compared to more downmarket stores.

'But I'm a Waitrose kind of person.' 'I shop at Sainsbury's to impress my friends.' 'I don't want my friends to see me shopping for meat at this cheap market.'

The above are all comments I have heard from various clients whose money I have tried to save.

Shall we grow up here? No one who is worth impressing gives a brass farthing about where you buy your food. These are not prestigious restaurants. They are warehouses full of goods to sell.

Supermarkets

I am not against shopping at supermarkets. There is a current idea that we should shop at old-fashioned little shops which are portrayed as beacons of perfection with fresh produce and helpful assistants. Well, I recall the time before big supermarkets when the local little food shops were far from helpful and stocked mainly suet and gravy powder, plus battered old tins and bruised peaches.

Supermarkets have some unpleasant habits, as I hear from small suppliers, but they have transformed our eating habits and the quality of the food and service we expect, and we would be silly to forget it. You can get bargains from them. But they are too successful at selling. You always pick up more than you intended. If you are trying to economise, use sparingly or avoid a weekly 'big shop'.

Top Tip! If you need to feed a family on a tight budget, I recommend Iceland for the amazing quantity and quality of its food. Everything seems priced in multiples of £1 so that you can easily work out how much you've spent.

Smaller supermarkets often try harder on prices and special offers.

The Co-op is both cheap and keen on ethical policies towards food and suppliers.

Shops like Aldi and Netto don't have familiar British food brands, but their own – and they are wonderfully cheap. Take cash because some don't take credit cards, and bring your own carrier bags – they may charge for these.

www.fixtureferrets.co.uk is a brilliant site with all the latest cut-price supermarket offers and two-for-one offers. You can sign up listing the products you are most interested in buying cheaply – in our case, Ben and Jerry's ice cream – and it emails you when it has a good offer to let you know about, and even which freebies are around.

Small and local shopping

Small local shops have to be competitively priced compared to supermarkets or they would be blasted off the High Street. My local butcher and greengrocer are about a third cheaper than supermarket prices and bring in fresh produce daily. My greengrocer buys B-grade produce which may not be the identikit size and shape the supermarkets demand, but children delight in finding bird-shaped potatoes and carrots that resemble a little man.

Stock up with things like jam at events like local fetes, the Women's Institute sale or horticultural shows. You are benefiting the local economy.

Old-fashioned gorblimey open-air markets tend to be cheapest of all.

You can order basics like flour by the small sack from health shops. I find a sack enables me to feed my five-person family for months.

> **Top Tip!** When shopping at a market, never stop at the first stall offering a bargain price. You will find the ones in the middle offer the best value because they occupy a less convenient space and have to compete.

Don't forget 'pound shops' in less-grand neighbourhoods. They sometimes operate on what is called the grey market, snapping up bargains left in foreign docks because someone can't pay the duty, for instance. Usually, food, soap powder and kitchen rolls are sold three for £1, but you must take cash.

Check local specialist shops near supermarkets. If a supermarket is offering three cat-food boxes for the price of two, the local pet shop will probably come up with a better offer, and may deliver it free.

Buy eggs and veg from local farmers' markets if you can. My local one sells free-range eggs at 40p a dozen cheaper than the supermarket. But don't be romantic about these farmers' markets. They are sometimes not cheap and I have known them boast about selling on inferior quality produce rejected by stores, which people assume is organic and pay through the nose for.

JANE'S GOLDEN TIP

If you want cheap, top-quality eggs, keep your own hens. You do not need a cockerel to get eggs daily. You do not need lots of space. I keep hens in an old garden shed. I calculate that, including every cost of having hens, my eggs cost under a penny each, whereas the equivalent in Waitrose costs around 20p per egg.

Buying in bulk

If you have many mouths to feed and want to buy in bulk, investigate joining a wholesale club like Makro, *www.makro.co.uk,* or Costco, *www.costco. co.uk,* 01923 213113. Both require that before you join, you are a bonafide business owner or member of specified professions, for instance working in a hospital or something. You have to check before turning up. I know a woman who got her membership by claiming to be her friend's lesbian partner! Don't go to warehouse clubs if you don't need to. That is falling into the discount diva trap, over-shopping, tying up cash on bulk buying which you don't need to do, when you could use that to pay your bills.

If you are giving a party, try your nearest wholesale fruit and veg and meat market, which normally sells larger quantities for cash. You have to get up early!

For large amounts of meat, try a catering butcher – get your nearest from Yellow Pages. Or do a deal with your local butcher, asking, 'If I order enough sausages (or whatever) to feed 50 people, what's your best price?'

Some people like boxed fruit and vegetable delivery schemes from local farms. These provide fresh seasonal produce. But they're not cheaper, in my experience. The only saving advantage is that you don't go down to the shops where you are tempted to buy more than you need.

Save jars and bottles to make your own jams and preserved vegetables. Get a book from the library or try *The Basic Basics: Jams, Preserves and Chutneys* by Marguerite Patten, £6.39 from Grub Street Publishing.

You can get bargains at supermarkets and I don't diss them. Follow my insider secrets for saving money here.

How to save money on a big supermarket shop

One of my clients used her supermarket shop on Fridays as the highlight of the week. She would have a coffee after shopping and treated the whole thing as a social activity in itself. Supermarkets love this. That is why they often place their cafés at the end of the shop, when you're hungriest and buy more food.

It is natural to want to reward yourself for spending

what I see as 'downtime' – when you're out of serious action – in a supermarket by adding a few extra treats; but an electric toothbrush, a DVD, some coloured candles and a potpourri can soon add £50 to your bill.

If you have to shop at supermarkets, **avoid the smaller convenience branches** – often labelled things like Metro or Express – which can charge higher prices.

Shop at supermarkets in cheaper areas. Supermarket prices tend not to be fixed across the country. They can vary according to local conditions.

Take your loyalty card. The average family saves over £26 a year on food using it.

Buy food from the back of the shelf. It has the longer sell-by dates so you won't have to throw away anything uneaten by tonight.

Don't buy pre-packed fruit and vegetables. Put things in a bag yourself. You will save considerable sums.

Look high and low on the shelves. I don't mean make a long search! The items in the middle of the shelves, at eye-height, are the supermarket's most profitable. Cheaper things are placed on the top and bottom shelves.

Never pick things up from the ends of the aisle. They are put there to tempt you. A lot of expensive research goes into finding new things you might pick up, as this is a real profit hotspot.

Don't shop when you are hungry or tired. As I said before, you will increase your spend by up to 20 per cent on average and all you will get is fatter.

Hungry? Don't sit in the café. You know the food is the same stuff you are buying, but with a massive mark-up. Instead, go to the deli counter and ask for a free sample of cheese to keep your taste buds quiet, or graze on an item from your trolley (that's supermarket speak for eating it!). This is technically illegal so make sure at the checkout to show the empty wrapper and pay for it, saying, 'I suffer from sugar imbalance and needed something to eat quickly or I would have collapsed.'

Don't buy ready-to-cook meals. My tests found that they can be up to eight times more expensive and you get less in the packet than the raw ingredients bought from the same store. Raw ingredients are just as easy to cook – steak, jacket potato, boiled broccoli, or omelettes take a few minutes. No one needs to buy ready-cooked pasta.

Try not to buy ready-prepared anything. Business schools will teach marketing pupils the lesson of the 80p grated cheese packet. They are selling you perhaps two minutes of your own time at a massive mark-up. What would you do that's so valuable with that time? Watch TV? Is it worth it?

Don't assume that anything on a shelf or dump bin that looks a bit tatty is actually a bargain. It might just be put there to LOOK like a bargain but at the normal price, in order to shift annoyingly lingering stock.

Don't buy three-for-the-price-of-two offers unless you wanted the thing to begin with. They will clutter your kitchen, you will eat them, need big costly American fridges to accommodate them, and get fatter.

Don't assume that larger boxes are best value. I once heard a soap powder executive boasting that this isn't the case. It isn't the case with my pets' favourite cat food either. Check the small print on the edge-of-shelf labels to see the price per item/weight and compare this price with a different-size box to check it really is good value for money.

Shop later in the day, when prices are marked down. Supermarkets tend to begin marking down at 2 or 2.30pm after lunch, then have another mark-down at around 5pm, then 7.30pm, then late before they close. Leave your shop till late for the best deals.

Supermarket delivery services are convenient if you get special offers which waive the £5-ish delivery charge. You can always share the charge by combining a shop with a neighbour or two, though all food will be dropped off at one address, of course.

"

JANE'S GOLDEN TIP
Talking of coloured and/or scented candles, which I was earlier, you can save loads of money painlessly by ignoring these (not least

because they stain your table linen too).
Instead buy cheap plain white household
candles and sprinkle aromatic oil on your light
bulbs or paper napkins or base of glasses to
scent the room instead. Also buy plain and
basic paper napkins and towels instead of
expensive coloured ones, and decorate your
table in more interesting ways with flowers
I use ivy entwined around glass stems in the
winter, for instance. This is free.

"

If you find a special offer has run out, ask for a 'rain check' voucher entitling you to the same offer, even after it has expired in the shop. Tesco offers this. 'I used to work in a Spar shop and we did this, but if you gave out too many, you got fired,' a checkout assistant told me.

> **Top Tip!** If anything is damaged, phone and complain. They will waive the price.

You have favourite food, but don't assume that all the variant flavours cost pretty much the same. In my local supermarket, Ryvita Original costs 42p, but identical sized packets of Dark Rye are 54p and Sesame, 78p.

Knowing prices of basics like milk and bread does help you to think quickly in shops when comparing prices. To help you compare accurately, supermarket websites supply prices per kilo which you can use to check up, even if you don't order home delivery. Particularly useful when buying meat.

Buy turkey instead of chicken and rice instead of potatoes. They are cheaper.

Buy chicken pieces with the skins on and remove these yourself. They are about half the price of skinned chicken pieces.

You get about three slices more bread for your money by buying medium-sliced rather than thick-sliced loaves.

Buy dried pasta rather than fresh. You can save over £1 per pack and the dried stuff serves more. Some top chefs say that they prefer dried anyway.

Don't buy nuts from the snack counter, but the cake-making section where they are unsalted and tend to be cheaper.

Chop everything finely, the Chinese way, when you cook. Vegetables and meat go so much further and you use less.

Make friends with local supermarket staff. They may pass on their staff discount. It has happened to me.

Money isn't everything when buying food. Stick to your principles and pay more for ethically-farmed food.

Organic food is more expensive. Is it worth it? You have to make your mind up. Farmers I have talked to mutter grimly that chemicals like sulphur used on organic crops can be more harmful than synthetic, non-organic chemicals.

Lose your snobbery about fresh being better than frozen. As long as you get fresh fruit and vegetables, you can buy other things without suffering from scurvy or other distressing illnesses. Thank goodness for New Zealand, whose excellent tender frozen lamb tends to be discounted tremendously. I fed four of us and a large dog for two days on one leg of lamb at £5.99 and we felt we had done royally.

Check out tinned beans. Not baked beans but ordinary cooked beans. Added to casseroles etc. they really fill one up and are healthy. At three or sometimes four tins for £1, I don't believe you can get better value.

If you drink a lot of juice, UHT packs of apple, orange and cranberry juice cost around a third of the price of fresh chiller juices.

Eat porridge. It is incredibly cheap and filling.

Lose all snobbery about oil and especially pressed olive oil. Buy a huge vat of the stuff as cheaply as you can and use it bit by bit.

"

JANE'S GOLDEN TIP

Baby food seems incredibly highly priced for what it is. Perhaps they are playing on your natural parental concerns. However, don't leave your common sense at the door. Make your own baby food and drinks. For instance, baby apple juice and water costs 56p (Budgens); apple juice, £2 for three

*cartons in most supermarkets, tap water free.
Mash your own banana rather than buying
'banana puree' which sounds a bit posher
and is priced accordingly.*

"

Free food

You can pick up nibbles at deli counters. You can
also sample wine, free, at Majestic wine warehouses,
www.majestic.co.uk, 01923 298 200.

You can find that day's leftover food – things like lettuce
still in its plastic bags – thrown into bins outside some
supermarkets and also dumped by market traders
at the end of the day. I have seen groups of people
known as 'freegans' waiting outside supermarkets
and taking these with great delight.

More than two-thirds of homes buy bagged salad at
well over £1 a time, rather than buying the ingredients
for a fraction of this, cutting them up and putting
them in a bowl. Yet factory-washed salad is dipped in
chlorine, said to destroy some of the nutrients.

Growing your food

I reclaimed a small area of our garden for growing
vegetables and, although a rank amateur, last summer
I did not buy vegetables for my family of five for two
months, relying on my new harvest. According to a
recent survey by BBC *Gardener's World* magazine,
people who grow vegetables at home save up to £10
a month, especially growing them from seed. This is

easy in a heated propagator – the cheapest I found was at B&Q for £12.99. I have also grown tomatoes from seed in the plastic boxes which grapes and tomatoes are sold in.

Think ahead when sowing crops and don't sow all your seeds at once or you have a glut of the same thing. Go for cut-and-come-again vegetables. Lettuce, cabbage, peas and beans tend to magically reappear after you take some off the plant, and are particularly filling.

I can't say that growing fruit and vegetables is entirely free. You have to factor in the cost of seed and feed, plus your time. You can spend a fortune on gardening equipment, too. Try to borrow or swap as much as you can and get friendly with the local park staff, who will give you booty like bulbs they don't want for next year.

The money-saving plus of growing and making your own food is that these make excellent gifts for friends, who are delighted with your home-grown garlic or onions, at a fraction of the cost of a shop-bought house plant or bunch of flowers.

Grow your own food from seed on the windowsill if nowhere else. Swiss Chard is a wonderful vegetable, as you can use it raw for salads or cooked as a spinach-style vegetable to mix in with pasta etc.

If you want to learn more skills, volunteer to help at any of the following:

Any one of the four Royal Horticultural Society's gardens: Wisley in Surrey; Harlow Carr in North Yorks; Hyde Hall in Essex; or Rosemoor in Devon. For more details call Elysa Rule: 020 7821 3120.

Any of the 200 National Trust gardens. Call the National Trust's Community Learning/Volunteering Advice Line on 0870 609 5383 or email them on volunteers@nationaltrust.org.uk.

HDRA, the organic gardening charity, has lots of sites and opportunities for gardener volunteers plus mentors to help support potential organic fruit and veg growers. Mentors get free training courses at HDRA's Coventry HQ plus newsletters, handbooks and seeds. For information, email Joanna Lewis on *jlewis@hdra.org.uk*.

Cheap seeds. Harvest your own from flowers, usually by drying the heads in the airing cupboard and shaking them into a plastic bag. Seed exchanging is the free way to get new plants. Search under 'seed exchange' for groups. Try *groups.yahoo.com/group/ seedexchange*.

I recommend Alan Romans, *www.alanromans.com*, 01337 831 060, whose packets cost from 50p, free p&p for orders over £5.

Join your local allotment society even if you don't have an allotment. This will enable you to purchase basics like fish blood and bone meal much cheaper than at a garden centre. The National Society of Allotment and Leisure Gardeners is on 01536 266 576, *www.nsalg.org.uk*. The National Vegetable Society is another useful mine of free advice and special offers for vegetable gardeners. *www.nvsuk.org.uk*, 0161 442 7190.

Join a local gardening club or horticultural society for free plants, swaps and equipment sharing. Your library lists these, or try the Royal Horticultural Society – David Osbourne at the RHS can give you details of 3,000 affiliated clubs. 020 7834 4333 and membership on 020 7821 3000.

Do your research before buying fruit trees. The old adage, 'Plant pears for heirs' should tell you that they take a long time to bear fruit. Choose modern, fast-fruiting varieties and 'self-fertilising' trees rather than those that need a companion tree before they can bear fruit. Check the number on the label carefully in order to find the size of the 'grown-up' tree. This can be complicated. Seek advice.

You can find information about food growing wild or in the garden which you can eat – not just mushrooms – from Richard Mabey's classic *Food For Free*, published by Collins, in a pocket-size edition useful for outdoor forages. The cheapest I have found is £3.49 from *www.tesco.com* or order it free from the library.

Pick your own food

This is much cheaper, with added attractions like tractor rides to keep children happy. Plan what you are going to do with all that sweetcorn in advance, though. For your nearest pick-your-own farm, farm shop or home-delivery scheme from farms, check *www.farmshopping.com*, 0845 45 88 420.

Finding free food

Foraging and picking food can be a fun family activity. At the time of writing, we are drinking our way through elegant and delicious non-alcoholic elderflower champagne, made in a few moments from flowers outside the kitchen door, and I have also frozen enough elderflower cordial to last until autumn. For the price of a few bags of sugar and some lemons, we save £2.84 a week on soft drinks. I am about to pick rosehips and elderberries to give us an autumn soft drink for free.

9

Major drains on finances and how to save on them

Dressing

Each home spends, on average, at least £22.30 per week on clothes and shoes: £3.50 in supermarket chains, £6.70 in chain stores and £12.10 in other stores.

Take a silly spender, and you will find they have several wardrobes (never one) bursting with clothes. Clothes tend to 'creep' out of the bedroom until they take up the spare-room wardrobe and even the garages of some people's homes.

There are two kinds of expensive clothes. Good quality, that lasts and lasts – and clothes with the labels on the outside which advertise a fashion house to the rest of us. Buy the former, wear things for years and eventually they become fashion classics. If they are very distinctive and stylish, like Biba clothes, they do become very valuable. But this is an exception.

"

JANE'S GOLDEN TIP

If you feel like buying new clothes or shoes, search the back of your wardrobe or shoe store first. You will find a forgotten dress or pair of shoes similar to the new ones you fancied.

"

Charity shops

Georgio Armani told me that he drove around Chelsea looking at the street fashion for inspiration. The street fashion comes from charity shops. Shop at those in the most expensive areas near you for the best bargains, or try Oxfam's special designer shops – Oxfam Originals in very trendy locations like Covent Garden and King's Road, Chelsea.

Dress agencies

These are great ways to get some money back on expensive clothes you no longer wear, which the agency sells for you at a commission. You can also buy good-as-new clothes, shoes and accessories at prices which begin where charity shops leave off. For local-to-you agencies, try *www.localuk.com* and *www.fashionfizz.co.uk*.

Pandora Dress Agency, London's most famous dress agency in Knightsbridge near Harrods, is at 16–22 Cheval Placer, London SW7, 020 7589 5289, *www.pandoradressagency.com*. Also try The Dress B, 020 7589 2240 and Salou, 020 7581 2380.

Also try Designer Warehouse Sales, 020 7837 3322, *www.dwslondon.co.uk*, or the last day of London Fashion Week, at which you will find wonderful bargains for women, men and children as all the major fashion houses sell off their samples and accessories, including luggage. This fashionfest happens several times a year. *www.londonfashionweek.co.uk;* info/ticket line is 0870 890 0097.

> ## JANE'S GOLDEN TIP
> *You can never go wrong with antiques. Clothes, shoes, bags – they do not have to be expensive, but anything old is always right and is unmistakably classier than anything new (apart from food).*

Vintage clothes

You can buy vintage clothing from Steinberg & Tolkien, 020 7376 3660 and Rellick, 020 8962 0089. Trend-setting mags such as *Dazed & Confused* and *i-D* often source vintage clothing for their fashion shoots from Rokit, Brighton, 01273 672053, *www.rokit.co.uk* or *www.pop-boutique.com* with stores in Liverpool, 0151 707 0051 or Manchester, 0161 236 5797.

Christmas

A survey by Populus revealed that most people spend over £500 on gifts and one out of ten Northerners spends over £1,000.

A survey by Somerfield on 'the stress of Christmas' revealed that many women take glossy Christmas magazine photos as their standard of perfection and reproach themselves if they can't do as well. They wouldn't if they saw the other side of the camera. Lighter fuel is used to get a pudding or log fire to flare, and to get all the candles burning simultaneously on a table usually involves people hiding under it and split-second timing, especially if sparklers are involved. So buy ready-made gravy if it gives you more time to play with the children and admire their new toys.

"

JANE'S GOLDEN TIP

The principle of Christmas is 'something to make their eyes light up'. Their eyes will not light up if you have beggared yourself and are stressed out and exhausted. They will light up if you put sparklers on everything.

"

Some original gift ideas

Don't go 'Christmas shopping'. You will get into a panic, caused by others being in a panic, and overspend. Most mail-order gift companies will dispatch wrapped presents for you, so you can shop from the phone or on the internet in one fell swoop. The additional advantage is that some will send you reminders in time for next Christmas, so you don't even have to compile a gift list!

Never enter an 'I can give more lavish gifts than you can' contest. The loser will feel a failure. A book, even if funny and crass, is an 'intellectual' gift whose price is irrelevant, so find one book and give it to all. My current all-purpose gift is a huge and pretty bluebell-fragranced soap, £4, from *Willowherb.com*, 01788 540749. It looks more expensive than it is, and if you order over £20 of soap at a time, you receive extra gifts and chocolates which you can also send as gifts.

Scratchcards, enclosed with a card, are a great way of sending an acceptable but cheap gift and avoiding postage. The recipient, in my experience, is delighted – and several people I have sent cards to have won money and still purr about it when they see me.

"
JANE'S GOLDEN TIP
www.fivepoundjewellery.com *sells the most amazing glitz and glitter for a mere £5.* **"**

Send everyone the same gift. That way, you don't spend time wandering round the shops buying gifts on a 'one for me, one for you' basis, and thinking what people would like.

Buy gifts on a three-for-the-price-of-two basis In autumn, Woolworths has an excellent toy sale Superdrug is also great for these offers.

Personally I think store vouchers are a waste of money. You may have to pay extra for the gift card and people forget to use them. You can always make your own voucher for your time or skills babysitting, gardening or whatever. People really appreciate that.

Don't give teachers lavish presents. Get the children

to choose them. My son Charlie once chose an Action Man for his teacher on the grounds that the poor woman must 'need' this essential.

> **Top Tip!** Stuck for a gift for a man? Or for people living abroad? The small but sophisticated and witty magazine *The Chap* will probably entertain, with its campaign for a return to 'proper' clothes and louche behaviour (for women too). £10 annually; *www.thechap.net;* or write in a good old-fashioned way to Mrs Porter, The Chap, PO Box 39216, London SE3 0XS.

"

JANE'S GOLDEN TIP

Put your money where Christmas should be and buy everyone you know a gift which is not for themselves, but a donation to a needy person. Two charities offer practical help to people in this country and far away, from buying a fishing net for £5, to stocking an entire farmyard for thousands: www.sendacowgifts.org.uk, *01225 874 222 and* www.goodgifts.org.uk, *020 7794 8000. The gifts are witty and unusual and you can (secretly or overtly) theme them to the recipient, for instance a pig or bees to make honey. The recipient receives a card telling them what you have bought in their name and a warm glow. They cannot say they don't like what you have bought them!*

"

Silly gifts

Hawkin's Bazaar catalogue contains the best range of cheap, silly Christmas gifts. *www.hawkin.com*, 0870 4294000. Also look at *www.letterbox.co.uk*, 0870 6007878.

Home-made is best

Anything home-made or home-grown is more 'valuable' than anything bought in a shop. Make your own chocolates, biscuits, bread, jam, bottled fruit …

If you must buy something posh, make it inexpensive.

You still get the expensive-looking wrapping if you buy a nail varnish from the Chanel shop or a tiny handbag spray from Penhaligon's. Fiona Temple at the Daily Mail gave me this hint.

Christmas food

We are not in a food crisis. Don't buy too much food. The shops are open even on Christmas morning. Most people put on 5lb in weight over the Christmas holidays. No one will shoot you if you forget brandy butter or bread sauce.

If you are going to buy a turkey, leave it as late as possible. You will find birds marked down especially in places like Iceland. I once served chicken instead of turkey and no one noticed!

> **Top Tip!** Don't buy a whole turkey if you don't want to. No one will check up on you! Packs of the best bits are cheaper.

Crackers. Buy cracker pulls, mottoes and tiny gifts from *www.absolutelycrackers.com*, 01908 604751. Save loo-roll card board tubes or bits of thin card for the body of the cracker, and use paper napkins and sparkly bits of left-over wrapping paper to tie each end of the cracker. 'Make your own' cracker kits with cardboard outers are in my experience a waste of money as you cannot pull cardboard easily.

Giftwrap. You do save bubble wrap and all sorts of paper through the year, don't you? The alternative is to ask a florist if you can buy a huge roll of florists' wrap. I bought mine, which is very pretty, five years ago from a florists' wholesaler and it is only half-used-up. Alternatively, use newspaper or plain paper of any kind, even begged, clean, from the local chippy, or from printers who always seem to have surplus free or cheap paper, and spray with gold and silver paint.

Cards. Get your children to draw these. Or download images for cards free from websites. Dover Bookshop, 020 7836 2111, *www.doverbooks.co.uk*, sells wonderful books of instant clip-art that are copyright-free Christmas images to photocopy or cut and colour, such as 'Christmas Drawings' (£8.99).

I am told that there is little or no difference between posting first or second class these days – things get there pretty much at the same time. Don't blame me, though …

Table decorations. Cover the table with paper from a roll of lining paper which you don't have to bother to launder later. Scribble festive messages all over it, or if you have time, stick down images cut from magazines.

The tree. The best-value and cheapest trees will probably be from members of The British Christmas Tree Growers Association, 0131 6641100, *www.bctga.co.uk*.

Buying a root-balled tree to keep in a pot over several years may be a good idea. As an alternative, use long branches from a bush, sprayed or painted white, gold or silver, or buy these from a florist and hang with pretty things. Or simply buy some lights and drape them outside on the nearest tree. Of course, you have to plug them in!

> **Top Tip!** Cut a few inches off the bottom of the tree before putting it on its stand and keep it liberally topped up with fresh water to make it last. I add a little plant food.

Decorating the tree. This is not the time for expensive shop-bought decorations. Trees are a kind of sentimental family record of your evolving life. Go back to the original Victorian German tradition and hang anything that you find glittery or interesting, even little dolls or teddies or walnuts sprayed or painted gold; souvenirs you brought back from holiday. Anything home-made should take pride of place.

> **Top Tip!** Flashing lights outside, dancing Santas, singing doormats etc. are a waste of money, unecological and vulgar unless you are someone's sweet Granny or similar, in which case you can do no wrong and normal canons of decency and good taste are suspended (unless you are a wicked drug-dealing Granny, in which case go to Jail and do not pass Go).

Holidays

So often, I hear that people's financial troubles began when they couldn't resist a cheap deal to Dubai or New York, where they had to shop as it is so cheap. This ignores the cost of getting there and the fact that you are supposed to pay customs duty on your purchases from the USA, making those bargains rather less attractive.

Twelve million of us take on debt to pay for a holiday. Six per cent admit to becoming overdrawn every time they take a holiday. (Source: Credit Action.)

For most people, the benefits of a break wear off within 24 hours (survey, Adnams Brewery). As I mentioned earlier, I rather resent going away on the grounds that I haven't spent time and money on making my home comfortable, in order to transport the family to live in two cramped rooms and pay hugely for it.

To save money this year, stay at home and go out for weekends and days or stay with friends. Even camping can be expensive by the time you pay for the kit. At home, you won't have to endure tummy trouble, other people, crime, stupid souvenir shopping for all and sundry, and exhausting flights.

If you insist on travelling, consider the on-costs – the price of living when you get there. Thomas Cook's 2006 survey into the cost of holidays reveals that Goa remains the world's cheapest package holiday destination, with Bulgaria and Spain the best European bargains. However, if you take the price of a pint of beer, Brazil is cheapest at 79p. (Yes, but there IS the price of the air ticket to add in there…)

> **Top Tip!** If you just want to lie by the pool, choose a hotel offering an all-inclusive deal for food, drinks and snacks.

Stay away from home free, and meet congenial people, by joining *www.staydontpay.net*, 01227 470780. Members earn 'credits' by giving others free b&b in their homes.

My favourite places for cheapness are the Youth Hostels Association, who have palatial places, accommodate all ages with cars, serve excellent meals with wine and don't ask you to do cleaning. Internet-only offers can net you extra savings. YHA is on 0870 770 8868, *www.yha.org.uk*.

Also check the Landmark Trust for amazing places

to stay at reasonable rents, from a banqueting house to a castle in Scotland. 01628 825 925, *www. landmarktrust.org.uk*.

Don't be lured into timeshare presentations, even by the offer of a free weekend away. While I'm on the subject of thinking you will get something for nothing, don't believe scratchcards, phone calls, letters or calls that say you have won a holiday. Always ask yourself, 'What's in it for them?' The answer is, they want to sell you something.

Holiday clubs are a variation of timeshare holidays which promise a selection of holidays in return for a membership fee. I suspect many newspaper 'financial agony' columns would be short of stories if it weren't for some of these clubs, whose poor members soon find themselves short of a bob or two and seem surprised when the owner's address is a hole in the wall in an obscure Spanish village. Many clubs are quite respectable, I'm sure. They are just not for the thrifty.

If you are skint, avoid 'buy now, pay later' travel deals. You are unlikely to be able to afford them later, if you can't now.

If you buy a holiday over the web, be aware that some websites automatically add travel insurance unless you specifically click to take it off – a ruse called passive selling.

Don't click through from one travel website to another. Exit and go again to the second site. You may find the prices are cheaper as they don't include commission paid to the first site.

To calculate the real costs of your holiday, include pre-travel spending like vaccinations, equipment for skiing or water sports, insurance and clothes, toys and suncream. Then there is spending at the airport and transfers to the hotel.

Don't bother with travellers' cheques whose service charges, or whatever they call them, can range from £12 to £21. Take a debit card on holiday, as you should get a better exchange rate and withdrawals cost £1.50 usually, saving the cost of commission. Check the Nationwide Gold Debit Card which does not charge commission on purchases abroad (for more info, see section on credit cards on page 82).

Use *www.oanda.com* for fast currency conversions. Make a written exchange-rate table for yourself and family and carry it for rapid calculations in shops.

A bottle of Johnny Walker whisky works wonders in a crisis. I always carried one when I travelled for *The European* newspaper. It can get you tables in restaurants and rooms in booked hotels.

Don't change money in the hotel. You usually get a poor exchange rate. Use a proper bureau de change. Don't let the foreign restaurant write your credit card bill in sterling, either – they will 'load' the exchange rate.

Leave your mobile at home (if you can). You may

have to pay for incoming calls. If you want to use your phone abroad to phone your friends or family who are there with you, buy a travel SIM card which enables you to pay local prices. *www.sim4travel.com*, 0905 335 0336, a phone line that charges you 40p a minute.

www.dh.gov.uk is the government website containing the latest health advice for travellers anywhere, help with getting medical treatment and information about how to reclaim the cost of treatment and medicine if you fall ill or have an accident in Europe. You now need to get a free EHIC (European Health Insurance Card), using an application form from a post office. This can take a month to arrive, so apply early before travelling.

Save money by bartering. Think of the local conditions – the weather in off-season, and any shortages. Take a stock of tee-shirts with slogans in English and anything good quality, like thermal gloves, condoms and glossy magazines, to barter for goods and services and give as tips and small thank-you gifts. Battery-operated goods are not a good idea, as they rust.

> **Top Tip!** Always book tickets in the exact name written on everyone's passport or you may not be allowed to travel. Also remember to renew your passport at least ten months before it runs out. Many countries, including the US, won't let you in with six months or less on your passport.

It is worth paying £7.50 for the Post Office 'check and send' service – where the clerk gives your form and photos the once-over and points out any mistakes. It is easy to make these mistakes, especially if you have under-16s. Read the form very carefully indeed and then get someone else to check for you too.

Hotels. Booking and paying the hotel yourself may be cheapest. Check reviews of destinations and hotels at *www.tripadvisor.com* and *www.hotelshark.com*. *www.nextag.com* and *www.laterooms.com* allow you to make discreet internet-only offers of up to 40 per cent off room rates for over eighty nice hotels all over the UK. For cheap hotels, try *www.laterooms.com* or *www.lowcostbeds.co.uk*.

Personally, I prefer a real person to arrange everything for me. Then I know whom to blame. Internet travel agencies include *www.travelsupermarket.com; www.opodo.co.uk; www.expedia.co.uk; www.allcheckin.com* and *www.short-breaks.com,* 0870 027 6002. The advantage if you book a package through them, and the airline goes bust or something goes wrong, is that they have to reimburse you and help. If you click through from airline to hotel to car hire, you have not bought a package and no agency will take responsibility if things go wrong.

For cheap flights, try getting someone abroad to book on your behalf from their end. You can save hundreds if not thousands.

Cars

The average car costs £5,539 a year or £15 a day to run. (Source: Credit Action.)

Zoomy cars cost a lot more, and so do cars you think you are going to do up and sell for a fortune. So before you 'invest' in that Caterham, check the sell-by date. You can actually lose money by selling a 'classic' car after a certain time. Buy a diesel car which holds its value better and gives you more miles per gallon than petrol.

Don't buy your next car. Try leasing it. You will get a better deal for the same money and as you have a newer car, you save money on maintenance.

Save £10 a week on a typical car by converting from petrol to LPG using a government grant to subsidise the initial work, which can cost £2,000. Then save 40 per cent on petrol, up to £10 on road tax and, in some cases, evade the Congestion Charge. The car switches back to run on petrol or diesel if there is no LPG available. Find out more from *www.greenfuel.*

org.uk, 0845 490 0189 or *www.gastech.co.uk*, 0845 355023.

> **Top Tip!** Also try Trade Sales, 336 Bath Road, Slough, Berks SL1 6JA, *www.trade-sales.co.uk*, 08701 220 220 – rough and ready but incredibly cheap. Cut-price car websites include *www.broadspeed.com*, *www.oneswoop.com*, and *www.virgincars.com.*

Remove luggage racks and boxes, empty picnic boxes and any other surplus items you carry. They can slow the car down and use more petrol.

Develop money-saving driving habits. Don't warm the engine up when the car is standing, but drive slowly for the first few miles, and don't speed or brake a lot. Switch off air conditioning. You use up to one extra gallon of petrol in every 140 miles (two litres per 100km).

Open the air vents rather than the windows. You use four per cent extra fuel driving at 60mph with the windows open.

Check your tyre pressure. Low pressure uses more fuel.

> **Top Tip!** As a rule of thumb, supermarket garages are cheapest for petrol. However, *www.petrolprices.com* tells you where you can get the cheapest petrol in your area – simply by typing in your post code. This website makes

you aware of the best place to buy petrol along your regularly travelled routes, and updates you automatically when this changes.

"

JANE'S GOLDEN TIP

If you drive a diesel, investigate courses given at the Centre for Alternative Technology in Wales on converting your car engine to run partly on cooking oil. Friends of mine say they do this without converting, merely by adding cooking oil every now and again but I clearly cannot endorse this. There are tax considerations too – fuel tax is administered by Customs & Excise and you have to declare what you are doing and pay appropriately, but CAT's experts can explain it all. www.cat.org.uk, 01654 705950.

"

Giving lifts

There are two types of car-sharing, lift-sharing or car pooling: regular journeys and occasional one-offs.

If giving lifts to schoolchildren with your own children, you can legally claim up to 40p per mile for car-sharing passengers. Try *www.school-run.org* for information.

www.liftshare.co.uk, 0870 011 1199 aims to match drivers with passengers to share journeys to work, school runs or wherever you might be heading. The matching service is free and you share petrol costs directly with sharers. You could join a security-checked car-share scheme at *www.roadpals.com*, £20 p.a. Or become a passenger yourself and save on vehicle wear-and-tear too.

Also try *www.carshare.com*, *www.shareAcar.com* (for commuters), *www.234car.com* and *www. freewheelers.co.uk* which specialises in lifts to festivals and sporting events.

Your local LETS barter scheme also has members offering regular or one-off lifts. You can offer lifts through them or exchange a lift for something you have to offer, like babysitting or teaching a language, lending a long ladder, or massage skills. You don't exchange direct with the person offering the lift, all favours traded are placed into a common bank. Your local authority, library or *www.letslink.net* will tell you more.

Your local authority should have loads of information about starting a car-share scheme. *www.carplus.org. uk* and *www.nationalcarshare.co.uk* both give advice and support to communities, clubs and associations who want to begin one.

New ecological, economical cars

Which are the most cost-efficient cars? This depends on what you want. There are green fuels like bioethanol, biodiesel, LPG and natural gas; and there are green cars, which use rechargeable batteries to store electricity like giant phones, hybrid electric cars which also use conventional fuel, fuel-cell electric cars which have no engines at all, and petrol and diesel cars with good fuel economy.

The best-known sexy car is the Toyota Prius, a dual-fuel car; at £17,500. Try Lexus for executive green cars. Honda's Civic Hybrid 1.3 does over 60 miles per gallon (from £16,000). At the cheapest end of the market, the tiny Reva G-wiz costs around 1p per mile and works on electricity, with a 45mph top speed and a 48-mile range, no road tax, no congestion charge, and a list price of £8,299. Classed as a quadracycle, its insurance group is O. *www.goingreen.co.uk*

Citroen's C2 Stop & Start (£10,690) uses 15 per cent less fuel in heavy traffic, does 50.4 miles per gallon, falls into the low Band C car-tax band and has a Group 4 insurance rating.

Try *www.whatgreencar.co.uk* for ideas and recommendations.

MOTs

If you think your car is OK, call your local council to find the name of your nearest government MOT test centre to save up to £500 on needless 'faults' found by garages which also offer repairs.

How to get reasonable repair bills

Members of The Good Garage Scheme have a code of conduct guaranteeing fair play. Find a member via *www.goodgaragescheme.co.uk*, 024 76474069.

Never ask a garage to 'just do everything' or you will pay for stupid things like a rattling glove box needing, no doubt, an expensive new lining.

Car tax

In 2008, drivers of the thirstiest 4x4 cars will pay £400 a year in road tax. However, you can save this by buying a classic Jeep, from £7,000, as vehicles built before 1973 are exempt from road tax. Try RR Motor Services for such Jeeps, *www.rrservices.co.uk*, 01233 820219.

Insurance

Get some quotes direct using a typical insurance comparison service like *www.confused.com*, then ask a broker for quotes. They know obscure insurers and if you have a ding, will help by handling the insurance company for you. I saved hundreds on my car insurance – with exactly the same insurer – by going through a broker rather than phoning direct.

You can also save money by insuring with the woman as principal driver, if you both share equally. However, it is usually more expensive to insure one person to drive a car than for two drivers.

If you are a young driver, I recommend taking the Institute of Advanced Motorists' Advanced Driving test, available via most driving schools. Your insurance bills will be discounted.

I am a great fan of the Pay as you Drive insurance pioneered by Norwich Union. This saves loads of money if you are not a regular commuter and use your car irregularly, especially if you drive a lot on motorways.

You have to pay £50 for a box to be installed in your car, which also gives you add-on voice-activated navigation and emergency help if you want it. Then each month, the box tracks when and where you have travelled, and you receive an itemised bill. Charges vary according to when you drive and whether it's on an ordinary urban road, motorway etc. I find the bill useful in itself – I can think how to cut down my travelling even further by seeing a record of each journey.

Unlike many ordinary insurance policies, you don't pay the whole annual sum in one go. You pay a monthly fee for basic insurance (theft, fire etc) and an extra fee per mile travelled. I now pay 45p (yes) a month basic insurance, fully comprehensive, and a few pennies per mile for most miles.

> **Top Tip!** After an accident dispute has been resolved, don't assume that your insurer will automatically adjust your premium to give you back your no claims bonus. You have to tell them or you could lose hundreds of pounds.

> **Top Tip!** If you live in Leeds or London and only use a car occasionally, you can hire a new car instantly by phone or online for less than £4 an hour, including fuel, insurance, cleaning, servicing, maintenance and breakdown repair and with no congestion charge to pay. 0870 446 6000, *www.whizzgo.co.uk*.

> **Top Tip!** Helphire is a company you call after an accident – no membership needed – if it wasn't your fault. They will protect you from paying your excess for repairs by charging the other person's insurance for your repairs at insurance-approved garages, hiring a good replacement vehicle and dealing with the insurance claim. 0500 224455, *www.helphire.co.uk*.

"

JANE'S GOLDEN HINT

A parking ticket is only valid once it has been stuck on your windscreen, so don't let a parking attendant hand you one.

"

Cosmetics and beauty creams

It is not true that the more expensive the cream, the more magical the effect. I used to think up the names of magic ingredients for expensive creams, in my early career as an advertising copywriter. Research told us that the key age for remortgaging the home to buy a pot of hope is when a woman hits 30.

Some would pay a hundred pounds for a pot of strawberry yoghurt if it were relabelled 'makes your bottom smaller and your skin younger'. When the Shangri-La effect doesn't happen, the pot joins the rest on the bathroom shelf, and it's back to the beauty counter for the next expensive 'treatment'. Or should that be 'treat'? If this is you, recognise the signs and remind yourself that Marilyn Monroe's beauty secret was a layer of Vaseline, then a layer of powder, building up the layers to give her skin a translucent look.

How to look a million pounds on a fiver a month, if that

Direct Cosmetics offer discounts of up to 70 per cent on toiletries, cosmetics and perfume. If you can't find what you want, ask. *www.directcosmetics.com*, 0870 746 0040. Also try Stonelake Ltd in Guernsey, 01481 720053.

www.cheap-perfume.co.uk has a guide to discounts, including shops that sometimes sell off unused tester bottles at £1.

Find any department store cosmetics counter or Space NK (020 8740 2085, *www.spacenk.com* for branches) on a quiet day like Monday and say, 'I don't know what to do about my skin/lipstick/foundation.' (Not sticky-out ears, though; nothing they can do about those.) You will receive offers of free makeovers and samples.

Get top-quality beauty treatments free or for a few pounds, electrolysis, manicures and massage, from supervised beauty students at your local College of Technology or Further Education. You usually have to book ahead. It is nice to tip the student. For Colleges of Further Education visit *www.direct.gov.uk* and then search for FE colleges.

Have a hair-do free or very cheap by becoming a 'model' for trainee hairdressers. Ask at any trendy-looking local salon or try Saks, 01325 380333.

Make your own beauty aids – though remember 'natural' things like strawberries can cause allergies and always test ingredients on your skin 24 hours ahead. My favourite recipe book is *Hints and Tips from Times Past*, published by Reader's Digest, which you can order free from the library. The Women's Institute also has *Simple Solutions*, a booklet with beauty and cleaning recipes, for £1. 020 7371 9300, *www.womens-institute.org.uk*.

Glycerine from your chemist for a few pence is a simple moisturiser.

Soften your hands the Victorian way by rubbing them with almond or olive oil, putting on a pair of cotton gloves and sleeping in them. Baking soda – a few teaspoons in your bath – softens your skin, apparently. The herbs or other magical ingredient contained in expensive bath salts can be in negligible amounts to be of any real medicinal value, so strike those off your money-saving shopping list.

Baby oil or almond oil from the chemist – perfumed by yourself if you wish – is a cheap alternative to expensive bath oils.

More typical wastes of money and how to save on them

Couture baby clothes. A survey by the Prudential (July 2005) found that 80 per cent of British babies have designer clothes from Versace, Prada and similar. Twelve per cent have designer luggage. One mother was pictured in the Daily Express saying she would pay £3,500 for her one-year-old's clothes that year.

Babies can't read and giving them expensive clothes does not prove you love them more. They just need to be clean, warm, dry and cuddled.

Baby clothes are only the beginning. Research pinpoints 180,000 British children whose parents spend £20,000 on fashions and luxuries for them each year. Wardrobe favourites include £250 leather jackets and mini-Porsches that work.

A TV series, *Britain's Spoilt Kids*, featured the parents of a six-year-old who confessed that they regretted lavishing gifts including an electric guitar and scooter and a wardrobe of designer clothes on their son; he threw himself on the floor when he didn't get his own way and told a psychiatrist that he wanted new parents who could buy him everything.

Personalised number plates. Vulgar and a dangerous distraction to other drivers. A titled friend bought a matching pair of number plates proclaiming MILORD and MILADY for himself and his wife. He was teased about them so badly – teasing was perhaps an understatement – that within a few weeks he 'lost' them. If you have this amount of money to waste, see my comments about charity at the end of this chapter.

A wine rack stacked with bottles. Do you think this signals to your friends that you are a wine connoisseur? More like prize plonker. Most supermarket and off-licence wines are chosen to be quaffed around the time when you buy them. The longer you leave such bottles, the more the flavour can actually go off. If you want to collect wine, you need expert advice and proper temperature-controlled storage.

Warranties for appliances. One electrical chain used to make more profit from these than from selling appliances. Staff are keen to push warranties if they earn commission on them. These guarantees offer to repair your purchase free, and may add protection against accidental damage or theft.

However, most appliances come with a year's guarantee from the manufacturer, free. You are also protected by consumer legislation that states you can get a refund or a new item if the item is not of satisfactory quality or fit for its purpose for a 'reasonable' time, though the law never states what time that is. You may also have accidental damage cover through your house contents insurance policy. Your local council's trading standards officer will advise you.

A warranty will only save money if the appliance is likely to break down many times and cost a lot to repair, in which case, don't buy it. Eighty-one per cent of washing machines don't break down during the first six years, according to the Consumers Association.

Clubs you attend once in a blue moon. Golf clubs, smart clubs where vodka costs £200 a bottle … Don't tell me! You're a member of a gym – and I expect you bought the tee-shirt – but you never go.

I am here to tell you that joining a gym – and paying for it – does not equal becoming healthy. An average annual gym membership costs £372 in the UK. (Source: Sainsbury's Bank.)

One in five people uses their gym less than once a month. (Source: Mintel market analysts.)

Do some sums and work out how much it costs you per visit. If it doesn't make financial sense, leave or scale down your membership to a cheaper level – deals for using it in the evening are usually the most expensive, but if you are too tired, be realistic! Cancelling a gym membership is costly: normally, you are locked-in to giving three months' notice. But by stopping your £50 a month gym membership, you save £600 a year.

Trading standards officers tell me that they have a steady stream of people complaining about health clubs and their attitudes to cancelled memberships. I have a particular place in my prayers for Cannons Health Club in Cheam, who puzzlingly told me that they simply did not answer any letters. Nor, it seemed, did they read them. Therefore two letters hand-delivered, cancelling my membership, could not be found and they averred that my membership cancellation could not be proved – so I had to go on paying. I had to complain to their head office before it was sorted out. I pass this on as a warning. Personally, I should photograph or even video yourself handing them a letter and photograph its contents as you hand it over. Asking for proof, rather than taking a customer's word of honour, is becoming too common.

Local authority-run gyms can be just as nice, and allow you to pay per visit – typically, around £5 – with no membership fee.

Top Tip! Unlike standing orders, which you have to cancel at the bank, a direct debit can only be cancelled by the person you are paying. If you have problems with any club which refuses to cancel your subscription, and goes on drawing a direct debit without your say-so, ask your bank to query it. Under their fair trading terms, they put all the payments into a separate account until things are sorted out. This gives the company trouble and usually acts as a catalyst for them to straighten up and fly right.

> **Top Tip!** Save money by not buying your new gym's tee-shirt or other expensive equipment on sale at reception. You may not be a member for very long and you will look as if you're on the staff by wearing their logo.

If you want to get fit, walk up escalators or walk instead of driving. Play tennis for peanuts in your local park or go to the local baths for a few pounds a time.

If you feel like a little pampering from time to time, all gyms hold regular free open days and the most luxurious offer free trial memberships. Ask, or keep an eye on the local papers. Or ask a friend to take you.

Vitamin tablets. We spend over £360m a year on nutritional supplements (Well, I didn't. I don't know about you). Ignore pressure to take more of these from America and from beauty and health writers, who might as well witter on about this as anything else.

Children, pregnant women and elderly people or vegans on diets may need specific supplements. See *www.nhsdirect.co.uk* for advice or ask your GP or health visitor.

For the rest of us, supplements don't replace healthy eating, nor are they a quick fix. Personally, I can't see how they can help you deal with stress or pollution, as some claim.

Some supplements take weeks to have a significant effect. Advice from *www.dietician.com* says that you don't need a multivitamin supplement if you eat normally, unless you consume under 1600 calories daily.

The body is a wonderful thing. Take vitamins with a pinch of salt. If you feel ill, see a doctor and get tests and the right treatment. If you simply feel low, go for a walk or do something for someone else.

White carpets and white sofas. Talk about the victory of hope over experience! I know they look nice in adverts, but we are now in the real world.

Natural woven floor coverings. I speak from experience, having moved into a house covered in these. How I wish the previous owners had saved the money and put down dried rushes! They would have been less rough underfoot and easier to keep clean.

"

JANE'S TRUE CONFESSION

When five foxes invaded my bedroom, coming in through the cat door when we were on holiday, I got rid of my sisal floor coverings. It was an interesting insurance claim, including steam-cleaning a chaise longue where we found one fox lounging among the cushions, eating chocolates and watching the telly. (I lied about the telly, but the rest is true. OK, not the chocolates either but it had eaten enough cat food.)

"

> **Top Tip!** If squirrels invade your home down the chimney, as they can, and run amok, causing damage, try to glimpse them disappearing up the nearest tree trunk. If they are red squirrels, they are a protected species and therefore your insurance claim may be upheld. Grey squirrels are considered a pest and your insurance claim will be rejected.

Gadgets and gizmos. These are typical Saturday-afternoon shopping purchases, often made by bored couples out together who want to go home with a toy. You won't understand the instructions. The only person who can is the one who wrote them. Or perhaps not. Years ago, I wrote ads for Kenwood and read a research report claiming that people stop using machines once they put them in a cupboard. Use it or get rid of it!

Expensive and elaborate kitchens. When house hunting, I lost count of the number of kitchens I saw that I would describe as 'footballers' wives' kitchens. Invariably, the wife would spiel on about how she loved to cook. She may have talked the talk, but her kitchen did not walk the walk. Set amid burnished acres of empty worktop, was one tiny sink – when any family cook needs two deep butler's sinks. Backlit cupboards displayed gleaming crystal, when I needed space for food and everyday dishes.

There are basic points to check when buying a kitchen, like the quality of the drawers and hinges – which in an ideal world, I should swing on with all my weight before buying, as my kids do at home during 'ordinary' use.

My experience is that a kitchen is not better because it costs more. It is only as practical as the designer who planned it. Some young man purporting to be a designer once said to me, 'You don't really need a place for the kitchen bin, do you?'

Investments and collectors' items. For 'exclusive' read 'expensive'. Nothing advertised in a mass publication is a collectors' item, or collectors who know what they are doing would have already bought it. Including bits of jewellery.

Computers. Do you need to buy one at all? If you only use it occasionally, ask to borrow someone else's or ask that someone else if they will look something up for you and ring you with the answer, saving a huge amount of extra hassle. If you rotate round your friends, like King Lear round his daughters' palaces, you won't outstay your welcome.

You can use a computer, free, at your local library. If you enrol for any course (even if only half an hour and you didn't turn up) at a College of Further Education, this also entitles you to use the computers in their library. Or ask a friend if you can use theirs. Call Learn Direct for advice on colleges near you, 0800 100 900.

There are also internet cafés in most places – check in Yellow Pages – which charge a fixed sum for access per hour. The advantage to you is that you pay no overheads, have no tiresome helpline to hang on to, and no broadband costs. ***This tip will save you hundreds if not thousands of pounds and hours of heartache.***

OnSpeed says it accelerates your access to websites, making it up to five times faster to connect, without broadband. A subscription costs £24.99 a year – saving around £20 a month charge for broadband. *www.onspeed.com*, 0870 758 5859. NB: Make sure you have good anti-virus software – dial-up connections are targets for fraudsters who re-route you through premium numbers.

Nights out and entertainment

Lydia earned £900 a month and had few outgoings, as she lived at home, but was always overdrawn after the first week, as she spent so much money on clubbing. I advised her to sign up for an evening class in DJ-ing which cost a few pounds a week. She loved the course, saved money and developed a new interest.

Check your local library or your local authority on the internet for its adult education classes. They usually offer everything from fashion to French, with discounts for students, OAPs and those on benefits.

Tickets for shows or matches are expensive, with ticket agencies and even auction sites like eBay adding extra sums from 30 per cent to 600 per cent of the price. Top agencies Keith Prowse, Ticketmaster and See Tickets charge £4 and upwards per ticket, plus £5 postage.

Many theatres sell cheap tickets on the day, sometimes from £5. The Society of London Theatres' half-price TKTS booths in Leicester Square and at Canary Wharf sell tickets for London shows. You can see what is available at *www.officiallondontheatre.co.uk/tkts/today*. Savings can be as much as £30 per seat.

TV and radio recordings are free – a brilliant alternative to paid-for shows. Ask your local stations, or for all channels, including satellite and pilot shows, Applause Store offers free seats. 0870 024 1000, *www.applausestore.com,* or try BBC Audience Services, 020 85761227, *www.bbc.co.uk/tickets*.

If you like going round National Trust houses, you might like to know that there is always a free entry day each year. It varies from place to place, so call your desired place and ask.

> **Top Tip!** Find a booking agency that charges a fee per order, not per ticket.

Entertaining children. People complain about the cost of keeping children amused. Don't forget stuff on your doorstep like organised bicycle rides or walks. If you live within striking distance, London Walks – 020 7624 78, *www.walks.com* – offers a huge variety of guided walks seven days a week: mornings, afternoons and evenings. Children under 15 are free provided they accompany a paying adult (£6). Buy a discount Walkabout card and it's even cheaper. After all that walking, and education, they're too whacked to demand the usual complement of naff souvenirs and McDonald's.

You can cut costs on games, DVDs and CDs by buying from Jersey via supermarkets' Jersey websites, reached through their main websites and then looking for e.g. 'Tesco Jersey' on the top bar.

> **Top Tip!** Cinemas are cheapest on unpopular nights like Mondays. Orange phone users can get two for the price of one on Wednesdays.

If you want to stay in, a postal DVD service may be cheaper than buying or renting DVDs. Pay a monthly subscription and order as many films as you like.

www.screenselect.co.uk, offers the first five rentals free, no late fee, no postage to pay, £9.99 per month.

www.tescodvdrental.com offers a free trial and all Freepost DVDs, from £4.47 a month.

Finally, don't you dare to waste more money after reading this!

There are kids in Britain who have little to wear and raid dustbins for food, yet are not considered badly enough 'in need' to be taken into care. Their parents are drug addicts and inadequates. Please stop wasting your money and instead donate it to a charity that tries to feed them one meal a day. They are always desperate for new Christmas presents so that each kid can have one. Kids Company, 1 Kenbury Street, London SE5 9BS, 020 7274 8378, *www.kidsco.org.uk*.

Planning ahead – saving money over life's lumps and bumps

Fifteen per cent of people aged 18–24 think an Individual Savings Account (ISA) is an iPod accessory and one in ten think it is an energy drink. (Source: *creditaction.org.uk*.)

If few of us plan ahead properly for Christmas, imagine how foggy we are about major life changes. Getting married, giving birth or retiring are rarely seen through anything but a golden haze – with little thought given to what might lie beyond.

Getting married

In the short term, taxwise, you lose money. In the long term, you gain emotional and financial stability especially (sorry to say this) if you are a woman with children and you divorce.

The average wedding costs £19,595. Forty-five per cent of couples – 117,000 people – have not planned how to pay for their wedding before they organise it, according to stockbrokers Brewin Dolphin Securities.

Engagement rings

These days the average ring costs £1,100, according to a recent survey by the Woolwich. That is ridiculous. Engagement rings cease to be important once you have a wedding ring; and to walk around with a glittering, expensive and easy-to-remove accessory is a come-on to thieves.

When I wrote jewellery TV advertisements, research revealed that people buying engagement rings positively avoid trying to get good value. Like sending flowers and arranging funerals, it's not considered 'nice' to haggle over the price. I say: fooey to that.

Buy a second-hand ring – except they won't call it that, they'll call it 'antique' because that sounds a lot more valuable, and so should you, when you present it to your girl. Ask your mother or the other senior women in your family if they have any rings which they should like to pass on within the family. That creates a lovely link down the years – and this is what aristocrats do (rich people hate paying for things if they have them already...how do you think they got rich?!). You just need to find a nice ring box, which you may be able to get for little or nothing from a local jeweller.

Or if you want something new, go to London's Hatton Garden, Birmingham's jewellery quarter or any similar concentration of trade jewellery makers or wholesalers near you and browse around the shops. Ask a few to quote on the cost of making you a design 'inspired' by the ring design you like. And save a lot of money.

Cutting the costs of the wedding, or any party

Buy beautiful, but don't bankrupt yourself or Dad in the process.

Have small nibbles of food that go into the mouth without needing a second bite, or they ruin people's clothes, and guests can't talk while they are eating.

Ignore ice sculptures or chocolate fountains. They are expensive and vulgar.

You can get away with simple food if you have as your centrepiece an eye-catching chocolate cake – my faves are by Choccywoccydoodah whose 'ordinary' cakes begin at a mere £25 and can be personalised, but they will do you a cake taller than yourself covered in chocolate cherubs – and they don't melt, even next to radiators. Guests talk about those cakes for years afterwards and you can mention that all sorts of Hollywood celebrities have them. *www. choccywoccydoodah.com*, 01273 329462.

Saving money on bridal dresses

Don't panic-buy. Make an appointment and shop on Mondays, when shops are least busy.

Choose a dress which needs no alterations, but if you do need extra work, always take your wedding shoes – or the dress may look too long or short on the day.

Talking of shoes, no law says you have to spend a fortune on shoes worn for perhaps four hours. Find cheap sequined slippers or ballet shoes for a few pounds.

A plain dress will be cheaper and more chic. A wonderful bouquet is better value because it will enhance the dress.

Find a dress you like in a magazine. Take it to a local dressmaker and ask them to copy it. But don't let the seamstress buy the fabric. To buy online, try *www.fabricsite.co.uk*. My favourite suppliers are MacCulloch & Wallis Ltd., *www.maculloch-wallis.co.uk*, 25 Derring Street, London, W1R 0BH, 0171 629 0311 and Allans of Duke Street, *www.allans-of-duke-street.com*, 75 Duke Street, Oxford Street, London W1M 5DJ, 0044 (0)20 7629 5947.

Buy accessories like tiaras and posies at a craft shop like Hobbycraft, *www.hobbycraft.co.uk*, 0800 027 2387.

Mango Gems handmakes pearl and crystal wedding jewellery, from £1.50 for a twinkle pin to around £30 for a tiara. 01983 2431230, *www.mangogems.co.uk*.

Hire your wedding and bridesmaids' dresses for half their shop price, and you could afford a couture frock.

If you buy, don't bother to tell yourself that you will sell the dress on. The most you will get for a designer frock is a few hundred. Ignore silk – it is hugely expensive and may show every crease. You can find lovely inexpensive frocks at websites like *www. DirectDresses.com*.

> **Top Tip!** Phone around charity shops in posh areas asking them to let you know if they have any good dresses – they are quickly snapped up. The charity shops along King's Road, Chelsea have wonderful dresses.

Oxfam sells new and second-hand bridal wear, from full-scale wedding dresses to all accessories for everyone involved in the big day, at its dedicated bridal-wear shops. Here is a list:

95 Corporation Street, Birmingham 0121 236 7376

54/58 Darley Street, Bradford 01274 306700

5 The Bridge, Chippenham, Wiltshire 01249 447061

300 Walsgrave Road, Walsgrave, Coventry 024 76 448909

258/258a Telegraph Road, Heswall, CH60 7SG, 0151 342 8416

17 Terminus Road, Eastbourne, 01323 640731

22 Market Street, Leicester, 0116 2556455

358 Rayners Lane, Pinner, 0208 8669616

76/78 High Street, Shirley, Southampton. By appointment only. Call Sue Hutchings on 07969 668939.

Flowers

For the room where the ceremony is happening and the reception. Check with the wedding and reception locations to see if more than one ceremony is happening that day, and make sure you're the second couple in. In which case, you may find the previous couple say, 'Keep the wedding flowers.' Or propose sharing the cost of flowers between all the couples being married that day.

For the bride and bridesmaids, groom and ushers. Choose flowers that are in season to save hundreds. Get a gardening-mad friend or relation to grow special flowers for you. Ask for double what you need, in case of mishaps. Tie simply with raffia or ribbon to match an outfit, but taper the ends of the flowers for elegance. Or buy flowers to make your own bouquet and buttonholes, and add greenery from the garden. Practise making it by finding a book or going on a short floristry course at your local College of Education which may well have an 'arranging flowers for weddings' course.

Visit a wholesale florists' supplier – for which you need a business card or letter on business-headed paper explaining that you are buying for a large party – or wholesale market like New Covent Garden Market, London SW8 5NX, open Monday to Friday 03.00 to 11.00am and Saturdays 04.00 to 10.00am, 020 7720 2211. It is up to individual traders whether they will sell direct to members of public – not many are so-inclined unless you are placing a really decent-size order. It is not a bad idea to take cash, £10 notes, not £20, as these may not be accepted because of fear of fraud.

If you don't feel confident, ask at the local church, horticultural society or Women's Institute. There are lots of talented amateur flower arrangers who would arrange your bouquet for a small consideration or a contribution to an organisation's funds or charity.

Keep table settings small and low or people won't be able to see each other. A round margarine tub sprayed or covered in fabric or silver paper is fine as a base. Or save on flowers by decorating tables with photos of the bride and groom in the past. Run a caption competition: presenting a prize for the wittiest line will give the best man something to say apart from telling scurrilous stories about the groom.

See *Wedding Flowers* by Paula Pryke, published by Jacqui Small, £15.00, second-hand copies available from *www.amazon.co.uk*.

Getting the best prices from locations and caterers. For the best catering prices, don't marry on a bank holiday. For the best location prices, marry on a weekday between October and February.

JANE'S GOLDEN TIP

Weddings are not an exam in perfection and having all the bits like 'favours' on the table. (Favours? Inedible silver almonds do my teeth

no favours; I don't know about yours.)
You can do no wrong on your wedding
day even if things go wrong around you,
so keep it light.

"

JANE'S TRUE CONFESSION

I have been married twice. The first time,
I had all the trimmings and was married in
pink silk at an Oxford college. Years later,
I remarried. This time, it was a ceremony
for us alone rather than a social come-one-
come-all. We had very little money, married
mid-morning and asked the local Café Rouge
to open early for us, without charge, on the
grounds that we would be bringing loads of
guests. We ordered what guests wanted from
their normal menu: buck's fizz, cappuccino
and chocolate croissants. A real wedding
breakfast! We didn't have to pay thousands
for a venue or pay florists and caterers and
then clear up. Everyone was happy, and the
early start gave us plenty of time to travel
to the honeymoon hotel and enjoy the
lovely surroundings, rather than arriving
tired and late.

"

Divorce

The average cost of divorce and finishing a marriage is
£28,000 according to a Norwich Union survey.

An excellent short guide is *Fresh Start: A Practical Guide to Separating your Finances When a Relationship Ends* by Alison Steed, free from the Yorkshire Building Society, 0845 1200 100, *www.ybs.co.uk*.

Legal arguments cost you money. Resolve everything personally or through an intermediary and then get a court to rubber-stamp it. Resolution, 01689 820272, *www.resolution.org.uk*, used to be called the Family Law Association and is a group of lawyers committed to helping you divorce as 'peacefully' (i.e. without inflating the legal bill) as possible.

Websites such as *www.divorceaid.co.uk* or *www.divorce-online.co.uk* can be useful, as they offer free, practical advice.

> **Top Tip!** Do not use your lawyer as an agony aunt – they cost hundreds of pounds an hour.

Buying a home

Buy the best place you can afford in a 'good' area rather than a good place in a 'bad' area. You make your home easier to sell, and having lived in all sorts of 'good' and 'bad' areas, I can say from experience that a good local authority will offer things free for which you would otherwise have to pay, saving you hundreds on 'grudge' purchases that bad local councils make you pay for. Free wheelie bins, free bin bags for recycling or garden rubbish, free children's activities, all sorts of grants and clean, well-lit streets are valuable extras that you don't get in deprived areas.

" JANE'S GOLDEN TIP

There is always a top limit to the value of a particular house or flat. This is determined by its location, garage, garden and other factors beyond your control. Do not make the mistake of spending thousands adding luxury extras to a house, in the hope of making an extra killing on the sale price above its natural level. You will be wasting your money. "

The average cost of buying a home is £12,500, to buy a detached home worth £293,000, according to the Woolwich (2006). Much of this goes on stamp duty, the tax you have to pay. When looking at houses and arranging loans, you need to include this sum in your calculations as they ask for this money very quickly, when you have lots of other things to arrange, and your deal can fall through if you don't have the money lined up.

STAMP DUTY RATES

Up to £125,000	Nil
£125,001-£200,000	one per cent of the price
£250,000-£500,000	three per cent
£500,001 or more	four per cent

" JANE'S GOLDEN TIP

If you are selling or buying a house, you will make it more attractive by pitching the price just underneath the next stamp-duty band, e.g. £245,000, and adding a sum for things like curtains and carpets which will not be taxable. But tell the truth. You may be checked up on. "

If you house-swap with someone else, and the difference in value is under £125,000, you don't have to pay stamp duty, but in case things change, check with whoever is doing your conveyancing (that is, the paperwork, not the removals men!).

Buy or lease for under £150,000 in certain 'deprived' areas and you don't need to pay stamp duty.

But you have to find this out before buying the home – it seems they won't refund it if you pay in error (which strikes me as wrong – surely mispaid tax can be reclaimed and this is no exception?). However, to find out, phone the Stamp Taxes Helpline, 0845 603 0135 or see *www.hmrc.gov.uk*, enter the potential home's post code and use the Disadvantaged Areas Relief Search Tool.

> **Top Tip!** Never buy homes in new developments at the quoted price. Negotiate.

Removal firms, solicitors and estate agent fees are

all negotiable. You should always get several quotes and haggle. 'So and so offered me less', usually produces the desired result. Also check out fixed-price conveyancing fees, often advertised in Yellow Pages or on the internet. You do not need to live near a conveyancing solicitor to use him or her – you do everything by email and post.

When you move into a new home, you don't know what horrors are in store, so it is well worth buying an insurance policy that sends workmen round to clear drains and deal with emergencies. I suggest buying one policy rather than individual ones from the water company, gas company etc., as it seems easier and better value.

Direct Line Home Response costs from £7 per month with a five per cent discount for buying online: 0845 2461999, *www.directline.com*, or Home Call from £8.95, 0800 19520 33, *www.homecall.co.uk*.

"

JANE'S GOLDEN TIP

Keep the policy number and phone number somewhere outside your home. If you lock yourself out, you will know whom to call to get a glazier to take out the window so you can climb in.

"

Being a student

Student bank accounts. Ignore introductory bribes (sorry, I mean 'free gifts'). Go for the account that gives you the largest interest-free overdraft. Use a comparison website like *www.moneysupermarket.com*.

How to save money on student rent. Buy a property as a student let. Afterwards you can hope to sell it at a profit. You can take out mortgages together with your parents or family. Ask a broker.

Graduation. Many banks automatically swap your student bank account to their 'graduate account', but shop around, ideally for an account lasting three years with the largest interest-free overdraft. If you're earning and don't need an overdraft (this may be a fantasy but bear with me), you can use the zero per cent credit card trick of taking the 'free' overdraft money and plonking it in a cash ISA that enables you to make and take all the interest, tax-free. You can make several hundred pounds this way. Make sure that the ISA is a flexible one that allows you draw money out and that you repay the overdraft money in plenty of time. Allow two weeks.

Pregnancy

The key to claiming any pregnancy-related benefit is form MATB1 which confirms your pregnancy. Your doctor or midwife can give you this when you are 20 weeks pregnant.

Maternity benefits, allowances and leave are complex, and *www.directgov.uk* carries an excellent guide under the 'benefits' section.

You are entitled to 26 weeks' maternity leave, even if you have only worked for your employer for a short time, followed by 26 weeks' additional maternity leave.

For more information, check your phone book under 'Benefits Centre' or try *www.jobcentreplus.gov.uk* or the Maternity Alliance, *www.maternityalliance.org. uk*, 020 7490 7639. Or see leaflet NI17A – 'A Guide to Maternity Benefits' from the Jobcentre Plus.

If you don't qualify for Statutory Maternity Pay because you are unemployed, changed employer recently or are self-employed, you may qualify for the Maternity Allowance for up to 39 weeks. This can be up to £112.75 a week starting from the 11th week before your baby is due to the day after the birth. You need to ask a Job Centre or Benefits Agency.

> **Top Tip!** Sort out your claim as soon as possible, or you risk hitting cut-off dates, especially if the baby comes early and you are in hospital and can't think straight. If information-giving staff are impossible – as some can be – don't argue. Phone again another time.

If you or your partner are getting benefits or allowances including income support or pension credit, you may be eligible for a Sure Start Maternity Grant of £500. You can claim from 11 weeks before your baby is due, until your baby is three months old. If you are adopting a baby, claim within three months of the adoption, as long as the baby is still under a year old. You need the leaflet 'Sure Start Maternity Grants from the Social Fund', from the Jobcentre Plus office.

> ## JANE'S GOLDEN TIP
>
> *Check with your local benefits or tax office that your National Insurance is credited free for each week you receive maternity benefits.*

Fathers can take two weeks' paid paternity leave paid by their employers at the same rate as Statutory Maternity Pay – up to £106 per week at the time of writing. If your weekly earnings fall below £75, you may be able to get Income Support whilst on leave. For advice, phone DTI Employment, 08457 14 31 43, *www.dti.gov.uk*.

You should fill in form SC3 (SC4 for adoptive fathers) which self-certifies the fact that you are becoming a father. Once you have done this, employers are not expected to hassle you for further proof.

Child benefit

For the eldest child, Child Benefit is £18.10 per week and for each other child, £12.10. It lasts until a child is 16, or 19 if a full-time student. One of the glories of the welfare state, this tax-free benefit is paid to the child's parent or guardian, no matter how rich or poor, and a life-saver it can be. Download or complete an application form online at *www.hmrc.gov.uk*. Or pick up an application form from post offices, Job offices, Local Authorities, Inland Revenue Enquiry Centres or the Citizens Advice Bureau.

Other benefits

Nine out of ten families with children, including carers who are not parents, can get Tax Credits, which are not actually credits but payments.

Families with children can claim up to £545 (in 2007-8) and up to £1,845 for each child in the family if your income is under £58,175 a year or up to £66,350 if you have a child under one. There is extra help available if your child is disabled. You can order a claim form from the Tax Credits Helpline, 0845 300 3900.

The other Tax Credit you may be entitled to, if either you or your partner is working, is called Working Tax Credit. You need to tell 'them' your earnings and how long you work for each week. The benefits per year are £1,730 for you, £1,700 for a second adult, £705 if you work for 30 hours or more per week, up to £2,310 for disability, and for those over 50 returning to work, up to £1,770, plus up to £300 per week per child for childcare costs.

For more information, try *www.inlandrevenue.gov.uk/ taxcredits* or 0845 300 3900 or *www.direct.gov.uk*.

"

JANE'S GOLDEN TIP
Start saving as early as you can. Each pound saved in your twenties and thirties is worth

ten times the sum of a pound saved in your forties and fifties. (See my suggestions for alternative investments at the end of this book, page 214.)

99

Redundancy

To calculate how much redundancy pay you are entitled to, use the ready reckoner at *www.direct.gov. uk* - the section entitled 'Redundancy and Leaving your Job' which has clear advice about all these distressing matters.

The first £30,000 of redundancy money – should you be so lucky to get anywhere near this, which most people don't – is untaxed. The rest of your money will be taxed at top rate, unless the redundancy money is 'part of your contract'. You need specialist help from a tax expert.

Rather than seeking advice from a lawyer, ask your Trade Union (even if you haven't been a member). Also check your home insurance policy. Quite often, there is a legal expenses sum there which you can claim, to consult a lawyer of the insurer's choosing. As typical legal cases cost up to £15,000 and can cost much more, this is well worth it.

The care sandwich

You may find yourself looking after your children and your ageing parents or relatives. Or you may be in need of care yourself.

Having cared for my late mother, and helped care for a terminally ill friend, my feeling is that if you can care for someone at home, at your own home or near to home, with bought-in nurses and carers, they are happier and it makes money go further. Don't try to be a saint and do everything. You will work yourself to a frazzle. Try *www.caredirections.co.uk* for help. Look in Yellow Pages under 'Care Agencies' or 'Nursing Agencies' too.

"

JANE'S GOLDEN TIP

Hospital social workers can be mines of information about good care homes.

"

Sheltered accommodation is preferable to care homes. Sheltered developments have wardens who check on you daily, or will come when an alarm is rung.

The cost of care homes varies greatly but is crippling – starting from £310 to £500 weekly.

Nursing homes – with medical care – start at around £450 a week. Shared rooms cost less, but sharing with strangers can be distressing for the people involved. If the person needing care is suffering from dementia, you may have a long search. These homes can be hard to find, and can be even more expensive, especially if the person is violent.

It is a truth universally acknowledged, at least in my home, that if you go away for the weekend leaving an elderly person who seems OK, they will fall off a chair whilst cleaning windows because they didn't want to bother anyone. So I suggest getting from social services, free if you're lucky, or buying from *www.ageconcern.org.uk* 0800 77 22 66, a wearable alarm which connects with a manned phone centre which can hear them and summon you or the emergency services. This involves a monthly subscription. A more expensive Sat Nav tracker which you can wear allows you (or your pet) to press a panic button and be found by worried relatives, and your position shown by internet, text or phone. *www.buddi.co.uk*, 0871 4238756.

Who pays for residential care?

One old lady remarked to me how galling she found it that, while she scrimped and saved in her life, and now had to use her savings to pay for her care, others in the same care home had simply spent all their money and then got the state to fund their care.

To get Social Services to pay for your care-home fees, at the time of writing you need less than £21,500 in savings or capital and/or a regular income that would not cover the care bill that Social Services would pay. They will pay everything if you have £12,750 in savings, or £16,000 in Wales. If you own a house, there is a twelve-week 'property disregard' or something called a Deferred Payments Scheme. You need to check carefully – figures can change. They also check that you have not given your property away recently in an attempt to avoid paying, so don't do that. If your partner or relative lives there, it can't be sold for your care fees.

When trying to work out how much you can afford for a care home, distinguish between 'continuing NHS health care', 'funded nursing care' (FNC) and ordinary everyday care (i.e. help getting out of bed etc.). The National Health Service will fund nursing care for someone who is ill in a home, but that does not include paying for carers to help with 'ordinary' activities like washing or dressing. That is extremely unfair if the person has dementia and needs help with every activity.

> **Top Tip!** Things are different in Scotland where care is generously funded. Time for a move North?

To get FNC, an assessing nurse decides whether you need low-category help, medium or high. The National Health Service then pays the care home a sum to cover this – £40, £83 or £133. In Wales there is one weekly payment of £111 at the time of writing. That is taken off the fee for accommodation, food and personal everyday care.

If you are going to stay in your own home or have a granny flat in someone else's home, it is possible to get an occupational therapist to come, free, via the NHS, to make a list of helpful adjustments to be made to your home, like rails and bathing aids. If you have reasonable savings, don't imagine you will get these for free and hang on, waiting. Eventually they write saying that you will have to buy these for yourself.

Do you want to retire?

Retirement age for men is 65 and for women, 60, but this will rise to 65 for both sexes between 2010 and 2020. The average man lives 18 years after retiring and saves £123,948, while women live 21½ years and save just £59,393.

Can you afford to retire? Conventional pension wisdom advised one to aim for a pension of two-thirds of your final salary. This is unlikely, these days, unless you are a civil servant. Find your pension statements. Request a Retirement Pension Forecast telling you how much you can expect to receive when you retire from the Retirement Pension Forecasting and Advice Unit (RPFA) at 0845 3000 168 or by filling in form BR19 online at *www.thepensionservice.gov.uk* and then using the search engine to get to the forecast service.

The Basic State Pension pays from £87.30 per week. Higher sums depend on your National Insurance contributions.

The Second State Pension (SERPS) is a top-up to the State Pension, which you may get if you are someone's employee.

Pension Credit tops up your pension. Apparently if you are sixty or over, you could get a weekly payment of £119.05 if you're single or £181.70 if you're a couple. For information try *www.thepensionservice. gov.uk*, 0845 60 60 265.

> **Top Tip!** The Country Gentlemen's Association is an old-fashioned gentlemanly kind of place, even for ladies, and I like its approach. You do not need to be a member (or a man, or even to live in the country) to ask for its free independent personal financial advice. They cover every financial product, even business loans, and advice comes from a panel of top financial experts, including one who wrote the pensions 'bible' used by the financial intermediary industry. They will even come and meet you at home face-to-face without obligation. If you decide to buy anything through them, you get complimentary membership of the CGA, worth over £40 a year – plus a host of other discounts. 01985 850706, *www.thecga.co.uk*.

> **Top Tip!** Can't find or can't remember an earlier company pension? Try the Pension Schemes Registry, *www.essentialpensions.co.uk*.

When you retire, or after your 50th birthday, you may be able to take 25 per cent of any pension fund as a tax-free lump sum and re-invest the rest, or use the rest to buy an annuity, which is an income paid for the rest of your life. You pay tax on this annuity. You need to take advice from an independent financial adviser.

Alternatives to conventional pensions

Pension plans may give you tax relief, adding value to your savings, but they have performed abysmally. Look at alternatives. Investment bonds, ISAs, houses, or other forms of solid investments can be part of your retirement savings. You can invest, currently, up to £7,000 per year in ISAs and use the proceeds free of income and capital gains tax. You don't have to buy an annuity with this, unlike pension plan funds.

The family home

Or if you are over 60, you can stay in your home and look at a Home Equity Plan, a loan based on the idea that eventually, when you die, the house will be sold and the money repaid to the loan company.

Another name for these schemes is a Lifetime Mortgage. You should be extremely cautious about them and check for a No Negative Equity Guarantee, which means that you will never be liable to repay any money in addition to the value of your home. Otherwise, interest builds up and swallows the value of your home plus your savings. Saga's website, *www.saga.co.uk*, explains things clearly and offers an Equity Release Scheme. 0800 156256, reference 5077S for details.

If you need repairs, improvements or changes made to your home, check with Houseproud, run by the

Home Improvement Trust through your local authority. This helps anyone who is disabled or over 60 to get building work done and loans with a no-possession guarantee.

Personally I intend to milk the idea of being a frail old lady for all it is worth. Take advantage of special offers like those from Help the Aged for the over-60s, including travel insurance and savings accounts to benefit grandchildren.

See Help the Aged, *www.helptheaged.org.uk* (Seniorline on 0808 800 6565) or:

England: 207–221 Pentonville Road, London, N1 9UZ, Tel. 020 7278 1114

Wales: 12 Cathedral Rd, Cardiff, CF11 9LJ Tel. 02920 346 550

Scotland: 11 Granton Square, Edinburgh, EH5 1HX Tel. 0131 551 6331

Northern Ireland: Ascot House, Shaftesbury Square Belfast, BT2 7DB Tel. 02890 230 666

Thinking of retiring abroad?

Can you speak the language? No? You will never get a plumber to do what you want. You would be better-off looking at the cheap rates for two-month-long holidays somewhere warm, and shutting or letting your home while you are gone. Or you could move into a Travelodge, as one couple have, using early-booking discounts to pay and saving thousands in heating their flat.

As an EU member you can live anywhere in the EU. Consider exchange rates and currency restrictions abroad. Although you will receive your state pension, it may not go up if you live outside full member countries of the EU or if you are not covered by EC social security regulations, so check. The upside of living abroad is that you may be able to claim extra benefits from your host country, and we have agreements with unexpected places like Barbados and the Philippines, although you can't claim things like housing benefit as if you lived in Britain.

Ask for more information from the International Pension Centre, Tyneview Park, Newcastle Upon Tyne, NE98 1BA, or try *www.thepensionservice.gov.uk* and find International Pensions whose Frequently Asked Questions section is reasonably good.

To get free or discounted state medical treatment in the EU, you need form E121 from the DWP as above. France is introducing age restrictions and British under-50s will have to pay, so check. If you come back to the UK from an EU country, you are entitled to free medical care, but if you return from living elsewhere, I understand that only emergency medicine is free. If you don't know what medical help you are entitled to here when coming from abroad, try 0191 218 1999.

You still pay UK tax, but some countries have a 'double taxation agreement' with the UK, enabling you to pay less. Check leaflet IR121 from the Inland Revenue.

For more information, ask the Foreign Office – *www.fco.gov.uk*, 0870 60 60 290.

Offshore banking can minimise the tax you pay. All the big banks and building societies offer offshore accounts: HSBC is at *www.offshore.hsbc.com*, Barclays at *www.wealth.barclays.com* and Abbey at *www.abbeyinternational.com*. To find the web address of any UK bank or building society go to *www.financelink.co.uk*.

Dying and funerals

Specify how you would like to be buried in your will. It saves so much trouble. For inspiration, the best guide is *The Natural Death Handbook*, which has loads of cheap but lovely ideas. I cannot recommend this book too highly for anyone who is, or whose loved one is, facing death or a degenerative illness. Free online at *www.ac026.dial.pipex.com/naturaldeath/publications.htm* or as a book, £15-50 for credit card payments or £14.99 by cheque, which includes a free Advance Funeral Wishes form, from the Natural Death Centre charity, 0871 288 2098.

The useful IR45 leaflet '*Income tax, capital gains tax and inheritance tax - what happens when someone dies?*' is free at post offices and GP surgeries. There is also information on the website *www.hmrc.gov.uk*.

> **Top Tip!** The moment you die, your assets are frozen and this can prove inconvenient if there are immediate bills to pay until your house is sold etc. An elderly lady I know has put some money aside in a 'secret' savings account to cover her funeral and other expenses, in the

name of a younger person she can trust. That way, they can pay her expenses without waiting months to be reimbursed.

Being ill

Cutting the cost of medical care

If you have a chronic condition like asthma or eczema, you are entitled to buy aids to your health without having VAT added by the shop. This applies to anything from organic cotton sheets to adjustable beds and is 'self-certifying', i.e. the shop gives you a simple form to fill out, and keeps and deducts VAT at source. The only place I have found which insists on a doctor's note is Dreams, the bed superstore, which charges VAT and makes you jump through hoops by filling in forms, unnecessarily in my opinion, before it refunds later.

For a full list of zero-rated VAT products, and a simple declaration to download and sign for buyers and sellers, look at *www.hmrc.gov.uk* or call 0845 010 9000.

Dentists

NHS treatment costs have become simpler and, dare I say it, cheaper for the most complex work. All UK residents are entitled to NHS treatment. For your nearest NHS dentist, contact NHS Direct on 0845 4647 or the website *www.nhs.uk*.

You may have to wait weeks or months for an appointment. There are only three NHS charges. £15.90 includes an examination, diagnosis, preventative care, x-rays and scale and polish, and urgent and out-of-hours treatment. The next charge, £43.60, includes everything such as fillings, root canal treatment or having a tooth out. The highest charge, £194, takes in crowns, bridges or dentures.

Children, those on low incomes and expectant mothers get free treatment up to 12 months after the birth with form FW8 from your midwife or GP.

Private charges vary hugely and it is worth phoning around and asking. A check-up can cost £15 or £90 and there seems no rhyme or reason why. I queried one dental quote, for the suspiciously round figure of £3,000, and was told 'You wouldn't understand.' So I left.

Before signing up with a dentist, check their opening hours, emergency and weekend cover too.

Schemes you pay into each month.

Denplan is the largest of these. You pay a fixed monthly fee in return for regular examinations and any treatment including a hygienist. *www.denplan.co.uk*, 01962 828000 and enquiries 0800 401 402.

Dental insurance plans

You can pay monthly sums and get back the cost of private examinations and emergencies, or the cost of all work. Quotes vary spectacularly.

www.moneysupermarket.com offers a comparison service and quoted four sums to cover a family of two adults and two children, from around £11 a month to £43.66 from WPA to cover all work, plus a ten per cent discount for online purchase in the first year. 0845 345 5708 for a phone service.

Cash plans

Often offered by non-profit-making companies, these refund much of the cost of dental or optician's charges, medical treatment, screening for cancer, diabetes and heart trouble and a little cash if you are admitted to hospital. You can make a profit if you take out the right plan, as you are entitled to payments for having a baby, dental and optical treatments, health screening and physiotherapy, osteopathy, chiropractic, acupuncture and homeopathy, chiropody and allergy testing. You can cut premiums by around 20 per cent by persuading your union or employer to offer a plan.

Association of Friendly Societies, 020 7216 7436, *www.afs.org.uk*. British Heath Care Association, 0153 651 9960, *www.bhca.org.uk*. HSA, 0800 072 1000, *www.hsa.co.uk*. Westfield Health, 0114 250 2000, *www.westfieldhealth.com*. Healthshield, 01270 588 555, *www.healthshield.co.uk*. Bupa, 0800 600 500, *www.bupa.co.uk*.

Going abroad for medical and dental work

Luxurious, clean and air-conditioned hospitals staffed with well-qualified smiling staff and working equipment … it seems like a dream. If you go down this route for an operation, you have to add travel costs, not to mention the cost of getting up-to-date vaccinations and anti-malaria drugs before travelling, which can be a good few hundred pounds. *www.worldhealthcare.net* is a useful site to consult.

Vital Europe claims to save up to 70% off dental fees by operating in Budapest with an initial £25 consultation in Harley Street. Typical charges are £230 for a tooth veneer, usually costing £580 in Britain. 0800 075 4400, *www.vitaleurope.com*.

Try an established medical tour operator. For India, *www.meddicaltourism.com* has links to all the main companies offering medical treatments and recommended travel agents.

Choose a destination that is not too hot and stuffy during the time you are there. Bangalore's Manipal Hospital is considered a good choice in India, offering a health check for a sixth of the price of a British private hospital.

Take someone with you – hospitals usually offer an adjacent bed free, unlike British private hospitals, which charge sums such as £80 a night to sleep near the patient. Airlines may say that they will not carry post-operative convalescents without a companion.

Many foreign hospitals have tie-ups with British private hospitals for aftercare which may add to the cost, but the NHS will still come to your rescue, wherever your original operation was performed.

The congratulations zone

Go back to your budget planner in this book (page 6) and see how much you used to spend.

Write your savings here.

Daily total spent	……………………………………
Weekly total spent	……………………………………
Monthly total spent	……………………………………
Total saved	……………………………………

Now have that final chocolate/beer/bubble bath or whatever your treat is. But don't have the lot in one go!

If you haven't saved as much as you hoped – today is another day. Don't give up. Don't go shopping. You can only do your best. Analyse what went wrong and go from there. Email me if you want to.

At least once a month, read the personal money sections of any good newspaper for up-to-date news. Keep an eye out for better rates, especially for mortgages, loans, credit cards, gas and electricity.

Contacting me

You can email me through my websites, *www.smartspending.co.uk* or *www.smartsavingtips.co.uk* or write to me at: The Old Rectory, 15 Malden Road, Cheam Village, Surrey SM3 8QD. Telephone 020 8644 3855.

Appendix 1
Swamped by debt? Where to get professional help

A typical person owes at least £28,000 to ten different lenders before they seek help or another way out apart from soldiering on. From the way some advertisements put it, you would think that walking away from debt and starting afresh are a piece of cake. They aren't. Sensible planning and a bit of self-denial are your first solutions, but if you can't manage, because of some traumatic event like illness or divorce, it's understandable. You will get back on your feet, though.

There are three main types of organisation advertising help for the debt-ridden.

First, companies which pose as debt specialists but actually offer you loans – which could be consolidation loans (the ones which lump all your existing debts into one big debt at a potentially lower rate). *www.fool. co.uk* is reported to have found that three out of five people who take out this kind of loan generate more debt for themselves, but that means two out of five clear their debts this way. If you decide to do this, good luck, and don't borrow more than you need and then go on holiday.

The second type of debt specialist company may do the opposite – advertise as if they are a 'last resort' loan company. When you call, they ask you for a payment upfront – it can be a large one – in order to renegotiate your debts on your behalf.

I have seen one such company in action at their call centre and they were very nasty, pretending to 'take pity' on people and offering them 'now or never' deals, which were in fact their standard deal – behaviour they justified by telling me that this was for customers' own good.

They typically issue you with a special bare-minimum bank account, arranged for their clients with one of the big banks, so that you can live, and then they act as a buffer between you and your creditors so that you are spared the misery of opening endless demanding letters. They freeze interest so that your debts don't mount further, then ask you to pay in a pre-agreed monthly sum which they distribute to your creditors for an agreed time.

The third type of debt specialists are not-for-profit organisations and companies which will give you advice and the same kind of help as the ones I've discussed above, but won't ask you to pay them upfront. Their payments come from a mixture of donations from big banks, and, I believe, a commission on all payments you make back to your creditors.

Beware that some companies pose as charities or trusts – but act as 'feeders' to other companies whose fees you pay.

The three types of help available

A debt management plan. This is the easiest option, unless you are totally swamped. It is also confidential, so the world and his wife will not be able to know you're in trouble. Choose an organisation which will do this for free – see my preferred list here.

I suggest filling in the budget planner at the back of this book first, and listing all your debts before contacting any organisation. If you can't face it, ask someone else to do it for you, who is not a gossip. Don't leave any debts out. This common mistake is very irritating as it does not give the person advising you the true picture, means that you continue getting upsetting letters from the company you owe money to, and you will be short of money as your debt plan will not include the secret debt.

Your debt counsellor will do the sums for you and give you a letter which you can write to each company you owe money to, setting out the situation sensibly. Banks and other lending organisations do not WANT to see you go bust. They should agree to sensible repayment proposals. However, of course, they won't lend you any more for at least a while.

The downside of these plans is that interest may not necessarily be completely stopped and that if you don't stick to the payments, you could end up being made bankrupt.

An IVA – Individual Voluntary Arrangement. This is suitable if you have at least £15,000 in unsecured debts and at least three unsecured creditors. You have to pay the costs upfront – and they are quite high.

This formal repayment plan falls between a debt management plan, which is an informal arrangement, and a bankruptcy, which is very legal and formal. The benefit is that you are not made bankrupt – though an IVA is publicly recorded and your credit rating is affected for six years even if your IVA has expired before then. That will make future credit and loan applications harder.

You will normally be expected to repay your debts over five years (not the one to three years of bankruptcy). You may be asked to 'release the equity' in your home or other property (in other words, sell it or mortgage it further) to repay the debt. Unless your home and assets are specifically excluded from the IVA proposal, if you fail to repay as agreed, your home and other assets can be taken and you may be made bankrupt.

Bankruptcy. The last resort. If you owe £750 or more, someone can petition a county court to make you bankrupt. You cannot just ignore the proceedings or leave the country. You must co-operate. Preferably, settle the debt.

If you go bankrupt, you free yourself from the worry of overwhelming debt, but this is not like becoming a child again, with someone else doing all the hard work for you. You lose everything of any value, even a ring or a watch – sentimental value is not a valid plea to keep anything. You still have to pay your way, including child maintenance, after you become bankrupt – and you may find it extremely hard to get credit and function in all the ways you did before. See *www.insolvency.gov.uk* for details of how to make yourself bankrupt, saving money on 'services' to help you go bankrupt at a price.

My favourites:

- CCCS, 0800 138 1111, *www.cccs.co.uk*.

- Payplan, 0800 917 7823, *www.payplan.com*.

- National Debtline, 0808 808 4000, *www.nationaldebtline.co.uk*.

- Citizens Advice Bureau. *www.citizensadvice.org.uk*, *www.adviceguide.org.uk*. Your phone book or local library will give you the address of your local branch.

> **Top Tip!** Before talking to any of these organisations, check that you have exactly the right name. The internet encourages a proliferation of similarly-titled companies. If they are coy about telling you how they fund their activities, or suddenly demand a fee, try somewhere else.

JANE'S GOLDEN TIP

If you can't go on, do not hand back the keys of your house to your mortgage provider and walk away. There are awful tales in the financial press of building societies who sell your home at auction for less than it's worth, then wait a bit until you are back on your feet – then bill you for the difference between your mortgage and the price the house sold for. They are only allowed to do this for a certain number of years after you left, and if it happens to you, consult the Citizens Advice Bureau.

Appendix 2
The full ultimate budget planner

The Ultimate Personal Budget Planner

Costs

Expenditure per month £

Mortgage

Top-up mortgage or second-property mortgage

Mortgage saving vehicle/endowment policy

1

2

3

Council tax

Credit card/store card payments

1

2

3

Hire purchase agreements/car loan
(remember any catalogue repayments)
Loan repayments (incl. loans from friends and family)
Property/garden maintenance (incl. roof repairs, new fixtures, plants, landscaping – over 12 mths)

House insurance:

• buildings

• contents

• any additional/specialist insurance cover

Water rates

Gas

Electricity

Oil

Coal/logs

Landline telephone

Mobile phone

1

2

3

4

Internet connection/dial-up fees

Ink cartridges/paper/stationery/home office costs

TV licence/rental

Cable/satellite/digital fees

Life assurance and private medical plans incl. Denplan or equivalent

1

2

3

Life insurance
Pension contributions

1

2

3

ISAs/saving scheme/stamps/commitments

Overdraft set-up fees/interest on overdraft/annual credit card fee/banking charges

Car tax

1

2

Car insurance

1

2

Breakdown cover

1

2

Car MOT/maintenance

1

2

Running costs

- petrol/oil/antifreeze
- car-wash/vacuum/valet
- parking, plus congestion charges and speeding or parking fines

Train/bus fares/season tickets

1

2

3

4

School uniform

School meals/work lunches

After-school clubs/music lessons (per child)

e.g. dance, Scouts, Guides, swimming, drama, judo etc.

Pocket money

Child maintenance payments

1

2

Childcare costs, e.g.:

• nanny/aupair plus their living costs

• nursery fees

• pre-school fees

• private school fees

• tutor fees

• student loans

• kid's activities/birthday parties/presents for other kids/teachers

• courses during school holidays.

• misc. costs for books/school trips/PTA etc.

Clothing

1

2

3

4

Shoes

1

2

3

4

Beauty/hair/spa treatments (incl. products)
Housekeeping

- all shopping (food and non-food)
- drinks
- window cleaner
- domestic cleaner
- ironing service/dry cleaning/laundry
- milkman
- florist (incl. any special deliveries to friends)
- newspaper/delivery boy charges
- Christmas tips for bins/milk/postman etc.

Pets

- food
- maintenance/classes (grooming etc.)
- equipment/shows
- vet's bills
- insurance

Club/society subs

Mag/newspaper/online subs

Hobbies

- specialist activities
- weekend activities

Socialising

- eating out
- drinking/going out
- smoking
- trips out/admissions/snacks etc.
- weddings/funerals/christenings etc. incl. outfits/ gifts
- hiring films/music incl. online downloads

Private healthcare/nursing home

1

2

Dental costs

1

2

Medical prescriptions

Charitable donations (regular and collections)

Holidays

- cost plus travel insurance
- taxi transfers/hanging about airport
- specialist equipment
- spending money

- excursions and outings
- food/drinks/snacks
- souvenirs

Seasonal: Gifts and Entertaining (Christmas, Easter, summer bbq, halloween etc., incl. decorations)

Miscellaneous: sweets, crisps, coffees, chewing-gum – you'll be surprised how much you spend each time you stop for petrol or pop in a newsagents!

Anything else ...

And the other stuff ...

Are you sure there's nothing else? ...

THE BOTTOM LINE TOTAL £...........................

YOU CAN HAVE WHAT YOU WANT, by Michael Neill

COSMIC ORDERING FOR BEGINNERS:
Everything You Need to Know to Make it
Work for You, by Barbel Mohr

COSMIC ORDERING ORACLE CARDS, by Barbel Mohr

ASK AND IT IS GIVEN:
Learning to Manifest Your Desires,
by Esther and Jerry Hicks

DAWN BRESLIN'S GUIDE TO SUPERCONFIDENCE,
by Dawn Breslin

All of the above are available at your local bookstore,
or may be ordered by contacting Hay House (see last page).

HAY HOUSE PUBLISHERS

We hope you enjoyed this Hay House book.
If you would like to receive a free catalogue featuring additional
Hay House books and products, or if you would like information
about the Hay Foundation, please contact:

Hay House UK Ltd
292B Kensal Rd • London W10 5BE
Tel: (44) 20 8962 1230; Fax: (44) 20 8962 1239
www.hayhouse.co.uk

***

Published and distributed in the United States of America by:
Hay House, Inc. • PO Box 5100 • Carlsbad, CA 92018-5100
Tel.: (1) 760 431 7695 or (1) 800 654 5126;
Fax: (1) 760 431 6948 or (1) 800 650 5115
www.hayhouse.com

Published and distributed in Australia by:
Hay House Australia Ltd • 18/36 Ralph St • Alexandria NSW 2015
Tel.: (61) 2 9669 4299; Fax: (61) 2 9669 4144
www.hayhouse.com.au

Published and distributed in the Republic of South Africa by:
Hay House SA (Pty) Ltd • PO Box 990 • Witkoppen 2068
Tel./Fax: (27) 11 467 8904 • www.hayhouse.co.za

Published and distributed in India by:
Hay House Publishers India • Muskaan Complex • Plot No.3
B-2 • Vasant Kunj • New Delhi – 110 070.
Tel.: (91) 11 41761620; Fax: (91) 11 41761630.
www.hayhouse.co.in

Distributed in Canada by:
Raincoast • 9050 Shaughnessy St • Vancouver, BC V6P 6E5
Tel.: (1) 604 323 7100; Fax: (1) 604 323 2600

***

Sign up via the Hay House UK website to receive the Hay House
online newsletter and stay informed about what's going on with
your favourite authors. You'll receive bimonthly announcements
about discounts and offers, special events, product highlights,
free excerpts, giveaways, and more!
www.hayhouse.co.uk